The Grea

C000257082

Alex Brummer is one of the UK's leading financial journalists and commentators. After a long and successful stint at the *Guardian* he moved to be City Editor at the *Daily Mail* in 2000. He has won prizes both as a foreign correspondent and as an economics writer. Awards received include Business Journalist of the Year 2006, Newspaper Journalist 2002 and Best City Journalist 2000. His books include *Hanson: A Biography* (Fourth Estate, 1994), *Weinstock: The Life and Times of Britain's Premier Industrialist* (HarperCollins, 1998) and *The Crunch* (Random House, 2008).

The Great Pensions Robbery

ALEX BRUMMER

The Great Pensions Robbery

How the Politicians Betrayed Retirement

BUSINESS
BOOKS

Published by Random House Business Books 2011

2 4 6 8 10 9 7 5 3 1

First published in Great Britain in 2010, with the
subtitle *How New Labour Betrayed Retirement*, by
Random House Business Books
Random House, 20 Vauxhall Bridge Road,
London SW1V 2SA

www.rbooks.co.uk

Addresses for companies within The Random House Group Limited can be found at:
www.randomhouse.co.uk/offices.htm

The Random House Group Limited Reg. No. 954009

A CIP catalogue record for this book
is available from the British Library

ISBN 9781847940384

Mixed Sources
Product group from well-managed
forests and other controlled sources
www.fsc.org   Cert no. TT-COC-2139
© 1996 Forest Stewardship Council

Typeset by SX Composing DTP, Rayleigh, Essex
Printed and bound in Great Britain by CPI Bookmarque, Croydon, CR0 4TD

Contents

APPENDICES

To my father Michael and father-in-law Saul, two
nonagenarians who are a constant inspiration

Preface

In the spring of 1997 I lunched at a fashionable Clerkenwell restaurant in London with the burly and cerebral chief executive of one of Britain's largest insurers – Sir Peter Davis, the man from the Pru (who went on to be chief executive of Sainsbury). He was among a new generation of insurance chiefs who recognised the fast changing nature of the savings industry. Under his leadership Prudential would eventually move to buy the M&G investment and fund management group for £1.9 billion, so as to give its clients access to more transparent and activist forms of saving.

Davis had two issues on his mind. Britain's oldest insurer Equitable Life was in the middle of a crisis. The company had promised overgenerous guaranteed pensions to millions of clients. Inflation and interest rates were falling and Equitable had gone to the courts to try and limit its payouts to customers. Behind the scenes its managers were exploring a possible takeover by other insurers, with stronger balance sheets which could absorb some of the losses. Davis noted that Equitable was not alone in such exposure to guaranteed payouts but that it was more vulnerable. Unlike public companies – which have access to the capital markets – it had no means of raising new funds to rebuild resources should a crisis arise.

The second issue was New Labour's likely accession to power. Davis told me that Shadow Chancellor Gordon Brown and his advisers were using the services of the accounting firm of Arthur

Andersen to search for new sources of tax income. Brown was concerned that Labour's election pledge not to increase the higher rate of income tax above 40 per cent would restrict the party's options in government. The Andersen firm had been chosen as it was off Whitehall's preferred list of accountant-consultants because of criticism levelled at its work in Northern Ireland, where it had been auditor to the failed Delorean sports car firm.

As a major stock market investor and pensions provider Davis had privately been consulted on two tax changes. The first was a proposal to remove the dividend tax credit which allowed pension funds to receive the payouts by quoted companies tax free. It was a measure we would later learn was worth £5 billion to £6 billion to occupational pension schemes, the bedrock of Britain's system of retirement provision. A second, less controversial tax was also proposed on the profits of the newly privatised electricity utilities, many of which had fallen into foreign hands. They had become unpopular because they were viewed to be making excessive earnings and paying overgenerous bonuses to executives.

Both tax proposals, however, were highly sensitive in the run-up to the May 1997 election and would have been an embarrassment to New Labour and the putative chancellor Gordon Brown had they been published by the *Guardian*, where I was working as financial editor. It might have been one of the best scoops of my career, but for reasons explained in this book the tale never appeared.

The lunch was critical, however, because it stimulated my interest both in Equitable Life and occupational pensions. These were both subjects that at the time struggled to win attention on financial pages, which were obsessed with mergers and acquisitions, the comings and goings of executives, company profits and the state of Britain's economy.

Generally speaking pensions were considered a matter for the personal finance or money pages of national newspapers in which the focus was on the consumer, the kind of pensions available and the quality of delivery, rather than anything else. Occasionally – as at the time of the Maxwell scandal in November 1991 – pension policy became front page news. But generally speaking it was not considered a 'sexy' subject.

All that would change quickly over the next decade. Equitable Life would close its doors to new business, the dividend tax raid would lead to wholesale closures of occupational pension funds, and within New Labour there would be a 13-year-long philosophical struggle over reform and the cost of retirement. The generosity of public-sector pensions, and the contrast with the broken system of private provision and the paucity of the universal state pension, would become a cause célèbre.

As City editor of the *Daily Mail* since May 2000 I have been able to chronicle the political struggles of New Labour to deal with these events. As time passed, pensions had also become a vital aspect of traditional City reporting, of bids and deals in an era of swelling pension deficits. Growing interest allowed the reporting and commentating to spread from the financial pages to the rest of the paper.

Over the last decade no subject, including the credit crunch and great panic of 2007–9, has attracted such a large postbag. I have been fortunate, in writing about pensions, to have the support of my editor Paul Dacre, the wise advice of my colleague on *Money Mail* Tony Hazell, and access to the reporting skills of my former deputy Ruth Sunderland (now business editor of the *Observer*).

Much of the material in this volume was gathered during my daily reporting and commentating which gave me access to many of the key policymakers in pensions. There have been countless conversations with insurance and pensions chiefs – some still in office, several now retired. I am also grateful to many of the leading politicians engaged in pension policy who made themselves available to me, along with several of the leading pension regulators.

Special mention must be made of three people. They are the

indefatigable economist and pension campaigner Ros Altmann, who has been a constant source of counsel; Frank Field, a bold voice in the search for revolutionary change to Britain's social security system; and Adair Turner, who made time to talk about the work of his Pensions Commission, amid his hard labour at the Financial Services Authority in the aftermath of crisis.

I also have relied on a number of written sources, all of which are credited in the text or listed in the Bibliography.

The book could never have happened without the diligence of my university friend and former *Guardian* colleague Norman Hayden. He collected, collated and helped to organise a great deal of the material, much of it very complex. I am also obliged to my *Daily Mail* City Office personal assistants Jody Knowles and Edwina O'Reilly, who arranged many of the interviews and slotted them into my diary. Thanks also to my other City Office colleagues. Their strong reporting of pensions issues has made my task that much easier. Experts at investment advisers Hargreaves Landsdown kindly provided me with valuable case study projections.

Volumes like this do not suddenly appear. There is a huge amount of work behind the scenes. Jonny Pegg, of the Jonathan Pegg Literary Agency, saw the value of this project early on and managed to convince Random House, publishers of my last book *The Crunch*, of the value of this very different project. It could never have been brought to fruition without the brilliant and robust editing of Nigel Wilcockson. Publishers are sometimes criticised for being slow, but Nigel moved in record time to turn this from raw material into a proper narrative.

Last, but not least, I must thank my family. Much of this book was written while on summer vacation in Bordeaux. All of those present, including my daughter Jessica, son-in-law Dan and grandchildren Rafi and Natasha, were very tolerant of my frequent absences when at the laptop. My sons Justin and Gabriel have rescued me several times from computer and communications chaos and have been helpful throughout.

Finally, a big hug and much gratitude to my wife Tricia who helped see me through this and sacrificed several vacations. She has been terrific.

Alex Brummer
February 2010

The Grosvenor gang

It was a night like others in the plush penthouse suite of the Grosvenor House Hotel on London's swanky Park Lane. Wealthy Labour MP Geoffrey Robinson was playing host to the inner circle of politicians and advisers surrounding Shadow Chancellor Gordon Brown in the crucial weeks leading up to the general election of May 1997. The suite, tucked away at the top of one of the capital's glitziest hotels and overlooking Hyde Park, had become their nerve centre, witnessing confidential gatherings of Robinson and his like-minded friends.

These were relaxed, extremely convivial and often 'blokey' occasions where room service was kept busy and the alcohol flowed as the friends and colleagues revelled in each other's company, indulging in some late-night gossip while tucking into takeaways and watching football on television. Not surprisingly these soccer-mad politicos of the Brown cabal became known as the Hotel Group.

A highly ambitious, thoughtful politician, Brown had always played his cards close to his chest and chosen his friends very carefully. His hopes, fears and plans were for the ears only of a select band of trusted lieutenants. The way the Hotel Group operated closely reflected his desire for privacy and total loyalty. Gatherings at which he could plan with a tightly knit group of loyal associates in Robinson's eighth-floor fully serviced suite were exactly how Brown liked it.

This night, however, was far from usual for the group. For once, the light-hearted socialising and the pizzas-and-beer mood were put to one side, and a more serious mood prevailed. With the election looming, there was important business to conduct and some forthright discussion and swift decision-making was needed. The challenge before them was a huge one: how to raise money for New Labour's wide-ranging programme of reforms. What they finally decided to do that night was to have far-reaching consequences. They would decide on courses of action that would profoundly affect millions of British companies, investors and workers for years, even generations, to come.

Who were these men making such momentous decisions in such a carefully controlled way? Foremost among them was Geoffrey Robinson himself. An old political campaigner, the convivial but controversial multimillionaire businessman was Brown's right-hand man and cheerleader-in-chief. A Cambridge graduate, he had first been elected to Parliament in 1976, and during the 1980s had acted as Labour front-bench spokesman on science, trade and regional affairs. It would be true to say, though, that during his 21 years in the House of Commons his real interests seemed to lie more in building a business empire, and he showed a real ability to make money during his spells as chief executive of Jaguar and managing director of Leyland.

He and Brown had enjoyed a long and extremely close association, and when the Coventry MP resigned his Shadow Cabinet post in 1986 to start the engineering firm TransTec, Brown took his place. By 1997 Robinson was the proud owner of a £20 million stake in TransTec, as well as a slice of Coventry City Football Club and the *New Statesman* magazine. He had two mansions in the UK (his main home being in Surrey) and an estate in Tuscany, which Tony Blair and his family apparently used for their summer holidays. Tom Bower's critical biography of Brown states that Robinson 'financed Brown's last years in opposition'. The *Daily Telegraph* estimated the support that Robinson provided as 'more than £200,000 to pay for the specialist advice Mr Brown needed for formulating his tax policies'. This specialist and secretive advice came from the accounting firm Arthur Andersen (eventually put out of business by the Enron scandal in 2001) in the months leading up to the election. It certainly seems to be the case that Robinson helped fund Brown in the lead-up to the 1997 election.

It is easy to see why a certain aura of mystery and even glamour surrounded Robinson. He was one of Labour's richest MPs and a major donor to the party. He was admired by Brown and Blair for his business acumen and his ability to bang heads together. True, his career so far had not been without controversy: some of his business dealings had raised a few eyebrows. However, his credentials were impressive and, in becoming an ally of Brown, he seemed a natural for a Treasury job, a post he was to enjoy for just twenty months.

Another key player in the group – which also contained some top aides – was Ed Balls, the future MP for Normanton, West Yorkshire. Balls had read philosophy, politics and economics at Keble College, Oxford and joined the *Financial Times* in 1990. Here he met his wife-to-be, Yvette Cooper, who also became a Labour MP. After four years as an economics specialist with the *Financial Times* and growing involvement in Labour politics, he became an economics adviser to Brown. By 1997 he was seen as one of Labour's rising stars and in 1999 was appointed chief economic adviser to the Treasury, a move that led to him being dubbed 'the most powerful unelected person in Britain'. Elected an MP in 2005, Balls later became economic secretary to the Treasury and, after Blair's departure from government in 2007, moved up to become children and schools secretary in Gordon Brown's Cabinet.

By contrast, Charlie Whelan was much more of a rough diamond. The son of a civil servant, this former member of the Communist Party had been a foreign exchange trader in the City before becoming a union researcher. He was media savvy and had been Brown's spin doctor since 1992. The abrasive Whelan revelled in the idea of Brown's rivalry with Tony Blair and was said to constantly ask, 'Who shall we support and who should we knock down?' From the start, his vitriol was directed in particular at the Blair camp; Whelan would later be the voice of Brown's unrelenting warfare against his civil servants.

The Brown cabal was determined to get their man off to a running start as chancellor of the exchequer, should Labour win the election. They had ambitious plans, and to finance these plans they urgently needed funding. What they decided to do was to launch a raid on pension funds.

Up until this point corporate pension funds had enjoyed an important tax break: they could claim a tax credit. A pension fund receiving an £80 dividend, for example, could receive £20 of tax relief. This sum could then be reinvested in the fund to help build up an endowment for the future. The view of the Brown cabal was that the tens of millions of people who paid into such corporate pension schemes were over-privileged and that the pension funds could afford to surrender more cash to government coffers. They made the decision, therefore, that pension funds and limited companies receiving dividends would no longer be able to reclaim the tax credit.

It sounds like a dull technicality. The ideological implications, however, were huge. Throughout the 1990s a new-look Labour Party had reached out to business and sought to increase its electoral appeal to the middle class. Abolishing tax credits flew right in the face of this. It is therefore scarcely surprising that Brown's inner sanctum took the further decision to keep their plan hidden. Anxious to avoid any risk of a public furore, they agreed not to reveal it more widely. In fact, nobody else in the New Labour hierarchy – possibly even including leader Tony Blair – appears to have heard about the plans until some days after the party swept to power on 1 May. Robinson reveals in his memoir, *The Unconventional Minister*, that the tax plans were committed to a document that was locked in a safe in his penthouse suite throughout the 1997 election campaign. While it sat there those members of the Labour Party not privy to the secret went round the country campaigning on a promise not to increase taxes at all.

In the years that followed there would be much debate about the role and importance of the Hotel Group. Lord Turnbull, the then permanent secretary to the Treasury, at one point even denied its very existence: 'I have never seen evidence of a so-called Hotel Group. If it ever existed, it had ceased to exist by the time I got here,' he said. But, as the *Guardian* reported in 1999:

> There were tensions in the aftermath of the election, with allegations that crucial decisions were being made by an inner circle of Brown confidants in Geoffrey Robinson's suite at the Grosvenor House Hotel in London. Treasury officials, including the-then Permanent Secretary, Sir Terence Burns, were allegedly frozen out of policy-making decisions.

The Group clearly had considerable power.

In immediate terms, the abolition of tax credits gave the new government some much-wanted cash. But the implications of the deed were huge and went well beyond the purely ideological. Some inkling of possible repercussions came when, amid the greatest secrecy, the Brown team road-tested their ideas with the accountants Arthur Andersen. In a project codenamed Cascade, confidential papers were drawn up that pointed out that there were risks in what Brown and his entourage were proposing to do.

Thirteen years on and we can see precisely how those risks have turned into grim reality. By 1999 the abolition of the tax credit was costing pension funds £5 billion a year. It was also helping to undermine fatally the generous final salary schemes – the gold standard of pensions – which ordinary working people and the middle classes had come to rely on as the cornerstone of a worry-free retirement. Today many pension schemes are in tatters and millions of hard-working people face an impoverished and uncertain old age.

But there's more to it than that. Brown's decision in 1997 set the tone for the attitude of key Labour decision-makers to the whole pensions arena. As the years of Labour rule went by, pensioners and those saving for their old age found themselves consistently at the back of the queue when it came to government attention. When pension scandals and crises arose, Labour kicked the issues into the long grass. There's little doubt that this great betrayal of people's retirement hopes and aspirations will have an impact for generations to come.

The circumstances surrounding it deserve an airing.

PART ONE

Establishing

CHAPTER 1

Lloyd George and the great divide

Carpenter George Yabsley awoke well before dawn to a freezing Devon morning on New Year's Day 1909. Quickly getting ready, he dressed, eschewed breakfast and set off from his modest terraced house to walk down the road to the main post office in the coastal town of Salcombe. When the Salcombe postmaster arrived for work some time later, he spotted George standing alone with his cap in his hand, huddled in the doorway against the cold, quietly waiting for the doors to open and business to get under way. Touched, the official decided to open up at 6.55 a.m. and, as the town clock struck seven, paid out Britain's first state old age pension to a delighted George.

George more than deserved it. He had had a tough life, typical of many. With no schooling to speak of, he had started work when he was just seven and, after 68 years of hard daily graft, cut a weather-beaten, rather stooped and tired figure. Now, at the age of 75, as he clutched his few shillings, he could contemplate a weekly sum that offered well-earned rest in a longed-for retirement – cause for extra celebration in the Yabsley household as he and his wife approached their golden wedding anniversary.

Clearly, that January day in 1909, a century ago, when the Old Age Pensions Act came into operation, was momentous for George and for the half a million other elderly men and women like him. The weekly payments they received – ranging from one shilling to five shillings – represented the chance to end a near-lifetime of often-gruelling work and took the edge off the worst of their poverty. One elderly lady summed up the feelings of those turning up at post offices throughout the country, when she remarked, 'I have been very poor, but now I am all right.'

The Old Age Pensions Act 1908, devised by Liberal Chancellor of the Exchequer David Lloyd George, introduced weekly non-contributory payments on a means-tested basis for those of good character aged 70 and over who earned less than £21 a year. Since average life expectancy for men at the time was a mere 48 years, this was scarcely generous. It did, however, establish some massively important principles that still resonate a century later.

First of all, Lloyd George's act acknowledged for the first time that the state had an obligation to provide a safety net for the elderly living close to or below the poverty line. Second, in order to control costs, estimated at £7.5 million, the act introduced the idea of means testing – an issue that would become ferociously controversial a hundred years later – to ensure that pension payments were confined to the neediest and that the cost to the Exchequer was kept under strict control.

The introduction of the first state pension may have been a key moment in the history of Britain's welfare state, but the idea of a pension – a sum provided for men and women to provide a living income when they stopped working – had actually existed in the British Isles since medieval times. The occupational pension, the forerunner of the large-scale private-sector schemes offered by employers of all sizes, was available in a variety of ways to a privileged few. You could get a retirement pension as a clergyman, for military service, as a civil servant, for service in a great household, by purchase from a monastery, as a member of a craft guild, or from a contract with a younger member of your family. The idea of a wage beyond retirement for years of service rendered was deeply rooted in the national culture and a valued part of the employment package.

The first of these occupational schemes, known as the Chatham

Chest, was founded in 1590 and used to pay pensions to injured sailors. It was financed by a deduction of sixpence (2.5p) a month from the seamen's wages. By 1660 the Chatham Chest was in serious financial difficulties as the number of pensioners surged during the First Dutch War against Spain. In 1667, a harbinger of things to come, the Chatham Chest ran out of money following poor investment decisions and the Great Fire of London, and had to be bailed out by the government. This was the first time the state recognised that it had a role to play in making sure that those people who had been prudent enough to put money aside for the future – as well as, in this case, serving the nation on the high seas – were properly protected.

Variations on the Chatham Chest idea started around this time. Among the innovations were so-called perpetual pensions, freely granted to favourites of the monarch or to reward others for political services, which were a charge on the Crown revenues. These, it could be argued, were the precursor of the generous public-sector pensions which have been paid to MPs, civil servants and other government workers in modern times. Another variation came in the 1670s with the first organised pension for Royal Navy officers – an extension of the Chatham Chest.

In the midst of all this, however, there was no concept of retirement at a fixed age unless workers had an employer wealthy enough to afford the cost involved. In effect, workers were required to toil on as long as they could. It was an early example of what modern critics of a rising state pension age describe as 'work until you drop'. Various Poor Law acts from 1598 to 1834 tried to alleviate the plight of the poor and unemployed, but the idea of some sort of national provision for old age never took off. It was not until towards the end of the nineteenth century that reformers began to agitate loudly on behalf of the elderly and, just as importantly, leading politicians started to take note.

Even at this late stage, despite the pioneering ideas of the seventeenth century, occupational pension plans were still rare.

Among the favoured few were civil servants and long-term employees of railway companies. Others in the private sector had to hope for a paternalistic employer – perhaps driven to help employees by strong religious beliefs – or one who set up a pension scheme to take advantage of existing tax rules. Among the first commercial schemes were those involving such well-known companies as WH Smith and the news service Reuters. Both developed pension provision for their employees in the 1860s.

For the aged who were also poor there was no such opportunity. Working people on low factory wages found it impossible to save or put anything aside for their old age. Moreover, industrialisation, by uprooting the rural population, had undermined traditional family structures and with them the network of informal support people had previously often offered to others. Thousands of people who moved to the cities to find employment in factories had no one to turn to for help. When they were old and unable to work, the only institution providing assistance was the grim and much dreaded workhouse.

By 1891 England had a population of just over 29 million, of whom 1.3 million were paupers. Among those, the over-60s accounted for 31 per cent. For most there was, to all intents and purposes, no prospect of retirement. In the 1880s 75 per cent of men aged 65 and over were working. As late as 1901 more than 60 per cent of men aged 65 and over were still active in the workforce.

Ironically, over a century later, we could be seeing a return to this state of affairs. Under proposals contained in the 2005 Pensions Commission report by Lord (Adair) Turner and adopted by the Labour government the state retirement age for men is destined to rise from 65 to 66 years in 2026 and to 68 by 2050. The Conservatives have gone one step further. In his 2009 party conference speech in Manchester George Osborne announced that the Conservatives would lift the male retirement age to 66 years from 2016 as part of a drive to improve the nation's public finances through long-term reform of pensions.

Back in the latter part of the nineteenth century, it had become increasingly apparent that there was inadequate support for the elderly. The 1890 report of the Royal Commission on the economic and social circumstances of the aged poor recognised this, revealing that a third of those in the workhouse were 'abjectly poor' due to a variety of reasons. Soon a reform movement was under way. A key date was 13 December 1898, when the Reverend Francis Herbert Stead, a Christian Socialist from Tyneside, convened a meeting in Browning Hall in Southwark at which Charles Booth, social reformer and anti-poverty campaigner, was the main speaker. This marked the beginning of a nationwide campaign on state old age pensions. The following year further conferences took place in Newcastle, Leeds, Manchester, Bristol, Glasgow and Birmingham. The state pension bandwagon was rolling. In 1902 George Barnes, general secretary of the Amalgamated Society of Engineers, formed the National Committee of Organised Labour for Promoting Old Age Pensions, to which thousands of trade unionists signed up. He spent three years travelling the country promoting social welfare reform to great public acclaim.

The National Pensions Committee called for a national campaign for old age pensions for all at the age of 65. They also demanded that those drawing a pension should not have to make financial contributions to the scheme beforehand – in other words a universal state scheme. Over the next decade the campaign managed to secure hundreds of thousands of signatures for its petitions, and persuaded Parliament to hold various inquiries into the viability of introducing a state pension scheme. Pressure for change was cranked up further in 1906 when a Labour Party motion advocating old age pensions was approved by the Commons. Labour was now at the forefront of the campaign for better retirement provision by the state, occupying the moral high ground on the issue – ironic, given what New Labour was to do nearly a century later.

Faced with the bleak facts of life for the aged poor and the groundswell of support for a pension system it was the feisty and radical Welsh Liberal Lloyd George who decided something had to be done. It was a brave political move: what Lloyd George had in mind flew in the face of much received wisdom. Late-nineteenth- and early-twentieth-century Britain, with its industrial muscle and growing middle class, had evolved an ethic that rated competition and personal achievement. British society, it was argued, was no longer based just on rank – although elements of the class system remained entrenched – but on free exchange, where anyone could achieve social and economic success. Such notions had been popularised by numerous books and articles in the nineteenth century – best demonstrated by the social engineer Samuel Smiles and his best-seller *Self-Help*, published in 1859. Smiles argued, along with others of his time, that individuals were responsible for their own future. According to this way of thinking, people's self-reliance would be fatally undermined were the state to become involved.

Lloyd George, by contrast, was heavily influenced by the revolutionary ideas of Tom Paine – especially his 1791 book *The Rights of Man*, which strongly argued for progressive taxation, family allowances and old age pensions, among other welfare provisions. A long-time opponent of Britain's Poor Law, Lloyd George was determined to 'lift the shadow of the workhouse from the homes of the poor'. Helped by a large Liberal majority in the Commons he put forward legislation to help those who were too old to work. To help pay for the scheme he proposed raising government revenues by £16 million a year as part of a Budget which increased public spending. The following year – 1909 – he returned to the fray with his People's Budget, aiming to raise additional government funds via increased taxes on alcohol, levies on tobacco and motor cars, higher death duties, and a new supertax of sixpence in the pound on people earning over £5,000 year.

The Conservatives were horrified, and while there was little they could do to block the Budget in the Commons they used their majority in the House of Lords to thwart it there. Lloyd George reacted by taking the case for a state pension to the country. He toured the nation, making speeches in working-class areas in which he portrayed the Tory peers as self-interested and privileged. He threatened to tax landowners. He even attacked hereditary membership in the House of Lords, describing his opponents as 'five hundred men, ordinary men, chosen accidentally from among the unemployed . . . on the principle of first of the litter'.

After a long stand-off, Lloyd George finally got his Budget through Parliament. It may have been limited in scope, but it represented the first real stab at tackling poverty among the elderly. It also marked out Lloyd George, Britain's last Liberal prime minister (1916–22), as the architect of Britain's state-run old age pension system, raising issues and problems that are still on the national agenda today. These included cost, an issue which the Washington-based International Monetary Fund is still concerned about; payout value, the source of endless wrangling in New Labour Britain; and age limits, the subject of current proposals to raise the retirement age. Lloyd George's introduction of means testing of income was also reinvented by Brown (as chancellor of the exchequer) via the creation of a pensions credit.

With the introduction of state old age pensions Lloyd George changed the whole nature of the relationship between government and the elderly. In effect the Liberal government was signing up to a new social compact which transferred responsibility for the elderly and those who could not work any longer from the charitable sector directly to government. Pensions would become a right for those who served their time by contributing to national wealth as part of the workforce. Winning support for state pensions was a struggle which required Lloyd George to take on the landed interests, but having won the battle there was no turning back. The state pension in one form or another was here to stay and ultimate responsibility for funding it now fell to government.

In 1919 the state old age pension was increased to ten shillings (50p). In 1925 Neville Chamberlain's Widows, Orphans and Old Age Contributory Pensions Act led to the payment of pensions for five years from the age of 65 for those earning up to £250 a year (after the five years, the 1908 scheme was deemed to apply, though without means testing). For the first time a formal state retirement age had been established; this would remain largely intact until Lord Turner's Pensions Commission proposed a gradual rise in the retirement age in its 2005 report.

In parallel, governments also saw the importance of self-reliance through occupational pensions and recognised that such schemes were a useful way to ease the burden on the state of old age provision. The 1921 Finance Act offered tax relief to pension schemes that satisfied certain conditions – a principle that would not be fully reversed until the 1997 pillage – and work-related pensions massively increased in popularity. By 1936 there were 2.5 million people in occupational schemes. For the employer they were a way of engendering loyalty among the workforce, their attractiveness greatly enhanced by the tax breaks involved. For the employee an occupational pension based on the salary he or she had earned during their working life was both a form of deferred salary earned through long service and a guarantee for the future. It was one of the greatest social welfare developments of the twentieth century.

It was a development that policymakers found irresistible. The bigger and better the tax breaks, the more companies and their workers were willing to save for retirement. And the stronger the occupational schemes, the less funding governments had to commit directly to state pensions. Successive governments, of all political stripes, recognised the usefulness of tax breaks in encouraging pensions saving by those in work and how such saving could relieve the burden on the state for future generations.

This was just as well because the severity of unemployment in the 1930s led politicians to question whether state pensions – which had now been around for just over two decades – were really sustainable. In calculations about their adequacy for the task, demographics also had to be taken into account, and in the 1930s there were real concerns about population trends. Statistics showed that the number of children in the average family in Britain fell from three in 1911 to two in 1940. On the plus side, this meant that there were fewer mouths to feed and clothe, easing pressure on household budgets in the short term. On the minus side and in the longer run, this decline threatened to undermine family income, particularly where there were members not working. Looking further ahead, it also threatened the very basis of state pension provision because there would be fewer people in the workforce paying the taxes needed to support the state pension.

As politicians, statisticians and Whitehall civil servants grappled with the figures, the private groups and public bodies that were springing up pressed for better state pensions. Advocates of improvements to the system toured the country speaking to packed halls and helped develop public awareness of the importance of improving provision for old age. By the time Britain went to war in 1939 there was a public appetite for radical pension reform.

CHAPTER 2

Building the welfare state

As German bombs rained down for the first time on wartime London, few could have looked beyond the immediate scenes of desolation and misery to imagine what peacetime Britain would be like and what its social needs would be. It all seemed a painfully long way off; staying alive and defeating Hitler was the limit of most people's ambitions. But, deep at the heart of Churchill's coalition government, a task force involving a select few from government circles – principally Minister of Labour Ernest Bevin – had been set the daunting challenge of planning ahead. Now, having carefully considered the issues and finalised preliminary details, Bevin was in a position to go public. Setting out from his office in Whitehall one day in 1940 his ministerial car weaved its way across the capital, managing to dodge a daytime air raid, to deliver him for a historic announcement of plans for post-war reconstruction.

It came during a speech in the unlikely setting of a weekly lunch meeting of the Rotary Club of London at the Connaught Rooms, just off Kingsway on the fringes of the Covent Garden fruit market. As part of the government's planning for life beyond the war, Bevin told his audience, Sir William Beveridge was being asked to produce a paper. Rather forbiddingly called *Social Insurance and Allied Services*, but better known as the Beveridge Report, it would be published in December 1942 and formed the blueprint for much of the post-war Labour government's sweeping welfare reforms.

Beveridge, the eldest son of a judge in the Indian Civil Service, was born in Bengal in 1879. After studying at Charterhouse and Balliol College, Oxford he became a lawyer. He later joined the Home Civil Service and in 1919 became director of the London School of Economics. In 1937 he was appointed master of University College, Oxford, a post he still held when, three years later, Bevin invited him to look into the haphazard existing social security system and make recommendations.

The Beveridge Committee began work in 1941, considering pension provision in the wider context of social reform. At that point Britain's pensions system comprised three elements: the 1908 Lloyd George non-contributory and means-tested scheme; the 1925 contributory scheme, which paid pensions for only five years from age 65, after which the pensioner proceeded to the 1908 scheme but without means testing; and a backup system of supplementary pensions paid to around 250,000 of the poorest pensioners.

In essence Beveridge's task was to unify the 1908 and 1925 systems, and to a large extent he succeeded. He believed that poverty stemmed not so much from low pay as from unemployment and old age. Making working people – however badly paid – contribute something towards the possibility of job loss or retirement therefore made complete sense. His report of December 1942 proposed that all those of working age should pay weekly contributions out of their wages. In return, benefits would be paid to those who were retired, sick, unemployed or widowed. He argued that this system would produce a minimum living standard 'below which no-one should be allowed to fall'.

After the Second World War, universal social protection became a central component of public policy all over Europe, and in Britain Beveridge's work laid the foundations for the 1946 National Insurance Act, a central plank in the nation's post-war reconstruction. But it was felt that physical reconstruction, such as new homes and rebuilding the country's infrastructure, had to take priority over wages and welfare benefits. Consequently the state pensions offered were modest, offering a basic minimum income to old people. Beveridge also argued in his report that in the welfare state the needs of the young had to come first:

> It is dangerous to be in any way lavish in old age until adequate provision has been assured for all other vital needs, such as the prevention of disease and the adequate nutrition of the young.

Helen Fawcett, writing in Jonathan Hollowell's collection of essays *Britain Since 1945*, says that Beveridge's proposals were based on a hard-headed view of work in which entitlement was predicated on a person's previous working record. Under the 1946 act, all British workers would have a basic state pension based on flat-rate contributions from employers and employees alike. From 1948, pensions would rise to just over £1 a week for a single person and just over £2 a week for a married couple, payable at 65 for men and at 60 for women. Life expectancy by this time had risen to 64 for women and 59 for men.

As with the 1925 act, the 1946 legislation assumed and encouraged a traditional role of women as wives rather than breadwinners. Married women in employment were allowed to opt out of the basic pension by making reduced National Insurance contributions, effectively discouraging them from contributing towards a pension in their own right. Marriage brought with it certain benefit entitlements which were deemed to compensate women for their exclusion from the labour market.

Understandably, the Beveridge legislation has been seen as a defining moment in the history of pensions in Britain. It made a non-means-tested basic state pension available to those who had paid National Insurance contributions as part of their taxes during their working life. Funded by government out of current revenues, each generation would pay for the pensions of its elders. The 1946 act began the quest of generations of politicians to ensure that pensioners should not be left too far behind as earnings grow, a quest that has inevitably created constant problems for public finances ever since.

This funding problem was exacerbated by the way the act was introduced. Beveridge had argued that the pensions should be phased in over 20 years – the so-called Golden Staircase – on grounds of fairness and cost. But Labour, under Prime Minister Attlee, decided to pay in full from the outset. It was a mighty expensive decision, although politically understandable in the immediate post-war period, when Britain was on its knees and needed a lift after six years of war.

There was also one unforeseen consequence that managed to become a thorn in the flesh of successive governments down the years. The act contained a clause that unintentionally penalised Britons who made the decision to retire elsewhere in the Commonwealth. Even though they had contributed to the UK's mandatory National Insurance scheme, their pensions were not to be up rated in line with inflation. Back in 1946 it was assumed that living expenses in sun-drenched spots such as Australia would not be as high as those for people struggling to survive in post-war Glasgow, Liverpool and other then very bleak areas of the UK. This anomaly would not be resolved for another 60 years.

Inevitably, Beveridge's blueprint was not without its critics. Some felt that the limits set were very low, forcing pensioners to live very austere lives. Others argued that in effect Britain was opting for a two-tier system, bearing the imprint of nineteenth-century welfare policy distinctions between 'deserving' and 'undeserving'. In the top tier, contributory benefits would go to the deserving, those with continuous employment records over a full working lifetime. The lower tier, those without such an employment record, would receive means-tested benefits. In the case of the universal pension this was made worse by the fact that the low level at which it was set – equivalent to 19 per cent of average male manual earnings in 1948 – meant that those without other income sources needed to apply for means-tested supplementary benefits.

That said, in comparison with pre-war times pensioners were clearly better off. Indeed the *Daily Mail* reported that Britain's poorest pensioners in the 1950s were actually more prosperous than their counterparts some 57 years on. In an article on 6 December 2007 it pointed out that in 1950 the state pension was £1.30 – 18.4 per cent of the average weekly wage of £7.08. By 1955 the weekly pension had risen to £2.19, or 19 per cent of the average wage of £10.55. But by 2007 the weekly pension had fallen to 15.9 per cent of average earnings. The fall in the value of the state pension was a result of the decision by the Thatcher government of the 1980s to break the so called 'earnings link' by which pensions were upgraded each year in line with average earnings. (Pensions of the Thatcher era and after have been linked to the Retail Prices Index, a measure that invariably lags behind the improvement in average earnings. Moreover, because the adjustment is based on the RPI in September of each year, it cannot be counted upon to deliver a reliable increase.)

But even if pensioners in the immediate post-war period were doing a bit better, genuine concerns grew in the course of the 1950s that the Beveridge reforms were not working well enough and that too many pensioners were still living in poverty. Many were unaware of – or reluctant to apply for – the extra support available. The elderly were happy to have more money coming in than they had in the 1930s and 40s, but the intrusive nature of and social stigma attached to means testing dissuaded them from topping up their money with additional funds they might be legally entitled to. National Assistance, as the top-up scheme was known, smacked to many elderly people of the Poor Law and charity, and they preferred to go without. As one London pensioner remarked, 'I don't want to tell people all my affairs. They ask too many questions. I'm proud, I suppose. The pension is different. Everyone has a right to that. But the other, they have to come round every six months or so asking questions.' The all-too-common result was the kind of scene witnessed by sociologist Peter Townsend. In his classic 1957 work

The Family Life of Old People he describes a visit to one poverty-stricken widow in Bethnal Green, east London:

> Her single room is a cold, desolate place, cheerless and shabby ... on a bitterly cold February evening she had no fire ... two boxes of Jewish biscuits were the only food in the room.

There were no further significant changes to the state pension under successive Conservative administrations from 1951 to 1958. Hugh Pemberton, a University of Bristol historian, believes that this lack of action stored up problems for the next decade. 'Because the 1946 settlement had resulted in a minimalist state pension locked in by contractual obligations,' he wrote, 'it had created the conditions for the development of a parallel system of occupational pension provision on a vastly greater scale than Beveridge had envisaged. As a consequence, by the mid-1950s, Britain effectively had two systems of mass pensions provision rather than the one envisaged by Beveridge; each locked-in by contractual obligations.'

For those relying on the new state pensions the position grew increasingly grim. Throughout the 1950s the Treasury sought to ease the burden on the national coffers by diverting social insurance contributions into the general exchequer. The public believed that they were paying into some kind of National Insurance fund which would pay for health care and their old age, but the direct link between National Insurance contributions and the services provided was severed. This was in line with the Treasury tradition, still very much alive in the twenty-first century, of placing fiscal prudence above all other considerations. Not surprisingly, the elderly poor found the going increasingly tough – and also felt increasingly isolated.

In the decade to 1960 and beyond the retired population was regarded as, if not exactly on the scrap heap, at least something of an appendage to the world of work. It wasn't until the 1980s and 1990s that leaving work came to be viewed more positively – offering possibilities for overseas travel, migration to milder climates, leisure and charitable and social work. In the post-war period those relying exclusively on the state were affected by a certain social stigma and had little cash to compensate them for this. There was a real social divide in Britain: workers on one side, the elderly on the other, and, within the elderly, another divide: those wholly reliant on state aid and those able to supplement state provision through private occupational pensions and a variety of taxpayer-funded public-sector schemes.

Change was in the air as the 1950s drew to a close. With the introduction of universal earnings-related pensions in Germany, the left in Britain argued that the welfare state was falling behind and the Conservative government was failing to act. For too many workers the flat-rate pension was seen as too low a proportion of earnings. In place of a flat-rate contribution, it was argued, better-off earners and their employers should be asked to pay more. In return, at least a proportion of their state pension should be earnings related.

In response the Labour Party proposed a national super-annuation scheme following a plan drawn up by Professor Richard Titmuss at the London School of Economics. This would create a nationally funded pension scheme, offering compulsory earnings-related supplementary pensions for all workers. The pension fund would be invested in equities under state management.

It was an idea ahead of its time, foreshadowing the 401k occupational pension plan in the US, the semi-compulsory pension plans in Sweden and Australia and the Personal Account (NEST), which would emerge from Lord Turner's Pensions Commission in 2005. It was duly included in Labour's manifesto for the 1959 general election and should have stood them in good stead. As Hugh Pemberton points out, the proposal was unusually well thought-out and could have been expected to play well electorally. In the event, however, the Conservatives stole Labour's thunder, taking action themselves in the lead-up to the election.

Initially, their plans were far-reaching. They saw that one way of satisfying the desire for an earnings-related element in pensions was simply for the private sector to provide occupational pensions for all, a solution pushed aggressively by John Boyd-Carpenter, minister for pensions. But they also realised that it was never going to be possible for the private sector to provide occupational pensions for all workers. There were too many people employed in small firms struggling to make ends meet, and placing an extra burden on them was not considered politically acceptable for the perennially struggling British economy. The inability of the private sector to deliver earnings-related pensions for all employees therefore necessitated an extension of the existing state pension. The question was: how far should it go, and how feasible was reform of the existing National Insurance pension?

The radical Tory thinker Iain Macleod, then minister of labour, with the support of the patrician prime minister, Harold Macmillan, produced initial proposals to compel employers either to set up and contribute to a private occupational pension scheme, or to enter a new state scheme of equivalent generosity. The Macleod proposal was ground-breaking because it recognised that the universal state pension needed to be bolstered for those people outside the occupational schemes provided by the commercial world and government. The concept of a supplementary state pension based upon earnings was established.

After considerable debate within Cabinet, however, plans for a root-and-branch reorganisation of the 1946 state scheme were eventually dropped. Instead, the flat-rate pension was retained and a separate, and not particularly generous, earnings-related or 'graduated' state pension was introduced. On the eve of the 1959 election the graduated scheme, with earnings-related contributions securing a higher pension on retirement, was created via the National Insurance Act.

This scheme covered only earnings of between £9 and £15 a week, so when the graduated pension was actually introduced in 1961 an important provision was made. National Insurance contributions from better-off employees and their employers would indeed be raised. However, occupational schemes and their beneficiaries would be allowed to opt out both of the higher contributions and of the extra graduated portion of the pension providing the pension offered was at least as good as the state scheme. A vital opt-out principle had been established that would add to the standing of occupational schemes.

By this time the Tories were less concerned with raising pensions than with increasing revenues to shore up future National Insurance Fund balances, so the contributions raised were well in excess of earnings-related pensions paid. In fact, the main object was to shift pension costs on to the private sector by encouraging occupational schemes to expand: employers who could promise an equivalent pension to the state scheme could contract out of the additional earnings-related contribution they would otherwise have to make to the state.

The limited nature of the new graduated state pension was in part the product of a continuing 'anti-state' culture in sections of the Conservative Party. By creating deadlock in the Cabinet at a time when the Tories knew they urgently needed to defuse the threat posed by Labour's proposals, opponents of a generous state earnings-related scheme, such as John Boyd-Carpenter and Peter Thorneycroft, the then Chancellor, were able to secure a decision to adopt a less ambitious scheme. Clearly, it was going to be inadequate in the long term, but Hugh Pemberton points out that, just as in 1945, short-term political expediency was thought more important than long-term effectiveness. As Macmillan told ministers, 'In the long run we shall all be dead . . . So, do not let us bother too much as long as we do not spend too much for the next two or three years.'

The decision made by Macmillan's government in 1959 was critical in the development of Britain's pensions system. Quite simply, it set the seal on the importance placed by central government on occupational pension schemes. The Tories had feared that if employers were forced to make higher contributions to the state scheme, the growth of occupational pensions might be slowed or even reversed. Now their continued growth was guaranteed.

Before the war they had been the preserve of a minority of around 13 per cent of the workforce, mainly public servants and higher-paid private-sector employees. Their number grew during and after the war, when the shortage of skilled labour made competition for workers acute and incentives were deemed necessary to attract and retain key employees. Now it was set to grow further. From the point of view of employers, occupational pension schemes could be used to secure well-qualified prospective employees, promising a form of postponed earnings. From the point of view of government, occupational pensions limited state liability and created funds that stimulated investment. When government did look at occupational pensions, it was generally only to tinker: the 1947 Finance Act, for example, limited the maximum amount of tax relief on occupational pensions and the proportion that could be taken as a lump sum.

Active membership of occupational funds rose throughout the 1950s. In 1953 it stood at 3.1 million. The following year the Phillips Committee noted that employers were becoming major providers of pensions. Three years later the government actuary reported that the proportion of workers in occupational schemes had leapt to 33 per cent, most of this growth having occurred since 1945. This rise was associated with a shift in the design of pension benefits from defined contribution to final salary (defined benefit) schemes.

Under the original defined contribution schemes workers received a pension based directly on what they and their employers had paid in over the years and the investment performance of the fund. The development of final salary, or defined benefit, plans sought to remove uncertainty from pensions provision by offering people a proportion of their final earnings on retirement. In many schemes the calculation was based on one-sixtieth of annual income over the working life, which could produce a pension of up to two-thirds of final salary. Defined benefit schemes became the norm, and the popularity of defined contribution and average salary defined benefit provisions declined from the 1950s to the 1970s.

The 1959 report of the Radcliffe Committee into the workings of the UK monetary system found that in the mid-1950s pension funds allocated around 20 per cent of their assets to the stock market. Ten years on this had more than doubled to 47 per cent. Britain's occupational pensions system was thus not only saving the exchequer money, but by moving the burden of provision from the state to the private sector, it was also directly contributing to investment in industry via the stock market.

Meanwhile, at the start of a new decade, and with the Macmillan reforms in place, the weekly basic state pension stood at £2.50, rising to £4 five years later. By then the Tories had lost office to Harold Wilson's Labour Party, but the pension story during Wilson's two governments, from June 1964 to June 1970, continued largely to be about the growth of occupational schemes. By the mid-1960s annual contributions under private schemes were offering significant sums for internal investment and underpinning the burgeoning London market for financial products and services. Retirement security was based on a virtually unfettered private sphere. Not surprisingly, British occupational pension cover grew to 12 million workers in 1966 and peaked at 49 per cent of the working population a year later.

Because occupational pensions were proving so successful, the Treasury showed itself very reluctant to impose any regulatory controls on their management. The fear was that government intervention might discourage employers from creating or sustaining them. The very simplicity of the schemes made them cheap and attractive to run. Index-linking was not obligatory, nor was cover for widows. But the lack of regulation carried risks. Many occupational schemes at this time were very small. In 1960, 75 per cent of the 40,000 private schemes in existence had fewer than 50 members. These were highly vulnerable if the employer went bust, particularly as only 50 per cent of occupational schemes were insured. Moreover, most occupational schemes did not offer index-linked pensions and some applied penalties to those who changed jobs. Many failed to provide cover for blue-collar workers outside the public sector.

The state pension remained largely unchanged in the Wilson years. On the surface this seems surprising. Wilson had come to power with all the dynamism born of his party's 13 years in the wilderness and with the image of a modernist reformer. His government had both the energy and the resolve to move the state pension story forward. Inflation had swiftly eroded the value of the new Conservative pension, which presented Labour with a chance for further reform in 1964. But what Wilson had not reckoned with was the full force of those determined to thwart him and in particular his plans for a universal, fully funded national state pension scheme (or superannuation fund), which would end the opt-out and offer employees outside the occupational schemes similar benefits.

Major employers and the financial services industry were against such a proposal because any move to abolish the principle of contracting out from the state system was deemed to threaten their business. Surprisingly perhaps, the Trades Union Congress (TUC) was also opposed. In general the TUC was more interested in supporting a higher basic state pension than in tackling earnings-related provision. Many unionised workers were in any case members of occupational schemes, and bolstering the value of these benefits was a prime goal. In the years of voluntary (and later statutory) income policies in the 1950s and 1960s, trade unions negotiated higher occupational pensions in partial compensation for wage restraint.

The biggest barrier to change, however, came from within Whitehall. Treasury criticism was, as so often before and since, both virulent and effective, and successfully delayed legislation for some time. In the event, Wilson decided to retain the contracting-out element of existing pension provision. Nevertheless his National

Superannuation Bill, by this stage sponsored by Labour intellectual and diarist Richard Crossman, fell when Wilson brought the general election forward and lost to Edward Heath's Conservatives in June 1970.

Wilson got one more crack at pensions when Labour returned to power in February 1974. This time, vowing to correct the failure of the 1961 Macmillan reform to keep pensioner incomes growing at the same pace as other earnings, he managed to get his Social Security Pensions Act through Parliament. It made two significant changes to the status quo. The first was to create a formal link between the basic state pension and earnings by instituting an automatic annual uprating. Barbara Castle, Labour's fiery social security minister, dusted down Richard Crossman's old scheme and increased the pension by 26 per cent to restore its value. The formula then applied was to increase pensions – which by 1975 had reached £13.30 a week – by a percentage equal to the growth of prices or earnings, whichever was the higher.

The second change involved the earnings related element of the state pension. In April 1978 SERPS – the State Earnings-Related Pension Scheme – was introduced. It offered for the first time a full-scale second tier to the UK state pension system. Now the earnings-related portion of the pension would be based on 25 per cent of the average of an employee's best 20 years of earnings. It was to be financed by an increase in the National Insurance contributions of both employees and employers.

The legislation had all-party support, though Conservative MP Nigel Lawson, who would be chancellor under Margaret Thatcher and later become a peer, thought the only justification for Tory support was to prevent pensions becoming a 'political football'. Crucially, however, the Conservative opt-out proposals of the 1960s survived. Occupational schemes were allowed to contract out of SERPS. Workers with adequate private provision could give up all or part of their SERPS benefits in return for lower National Insurance contributions.

Up until now a certain consensus had operated with regard to pensions. Labour and Conservative politicians might differ on the details, but the thrust of their plans was essentially the same. This was about to change. The first inklings of an alteration in Conservative views actually dated back to Edward Heath's government of 1970–4. But a full public airing had to wait until Wilson's Labour successor Jim Callaghan fell at the polls in June 1979. Now the Conservatives under Margaret Thatcher were in power, faced with tough problems and with a leader determined to tackle them.

Britain in 1979 was a basket case. The economy was ailing, and overall budget commitments greatly exceeded government revenues. Social security spending was a particular concern. In 1950 it had represented 5.1 per cent of national income; by 1965 the cost of pensions was twice that which Beveridge had predicted; and by 1979 it represented 8.4 per cent of national output, with pensioners being by far the largest group of beneficiaries.

Mrs Thatcher was an apostle of self-reliance. She believed fervently in a home-owning democracy in which people took pride and control over their own place of living. In the same way she believed that individuals should assume responsibility for their retirement provision. She was unhappy with the earnings link in the state pension. At the same time she wanted the national emphasis switched to private pensions.

Writing in the *Sunday Times* in April 2007 Labour MP Frank Field summed up the situation Thatcher inherited:

By 1979, occupational pensions had grown from the modest initiatives of the 1920s and 30s into the great welfare success of this country. Britain had more assets owned by occupational and personal pension schemes than the whole of the asset portfolio owned by other European Community schemes combined. And yet welfare bills continued to escalate in an apparently unstoppable fashion.

'Welfare,' he concluded, 'was about to undergo another major rethink.'

The starting point for Mrs Thatcher's reforms was to end the practice by which state pensions were linked to earnings or prices – whichever was higher. She noted that this tended to boost the state pension under all economic circumstances, during periods of both boom and bust, and that this seemed unaffordable.

Action came in three stages. First, in their 1980 Social Security Act the Tories removed the formal link that allowed pensions to rise in step with wages and instead linked the basic state pension simply to increases in prices via the Retail Price Index. This was a key decision and, although controversial at the time, is still in force. The Treasury in particular has favoured it because through much of the 1990s and the period from 2000 earnings easily outstripped price inflation, allowing pensions to be increased at a much slower rate than would have been the case if the old link to salaries had been preserved. Ironically, the issue has re-entered the political arena. The Conservative Party, which broke the earnings link in the first place, is now committed under the leadership of David Cameron and George Osborne to its restoration.

Second, in 1985 the government turned its attention to the long-term problem of the State Earnings-Related Pension Scheme. In the words of Lord (Nigel) Lawson, 'It was clear to anyone who took the trouble to analyse SERPS that it was a doomsday machine.' The Tories did not want to abolish the scheme as they thought the arguments for its creation were sound, but they did want to overhaul it. Taxpayers were to be given two options. Either they could remain in a somewhat less generous SERPS, in which the percentage of income paid out at retirement would be reduced from 25 to 20 per cent, or they could contract out. Until this point only employer-run schemes had been allowed to opt out of SERPS and make their own arrangements. From now on individuals would enjoy the same choice.

This new facility took the form of the personal pension. This was the third component of Tory pension policy under Margaret Thatcher. Individuals could save into it out of their pre-tax income and, if they opted out of SERPS, would also benefit from a rebate from National Insurance contributions. Indeed, for a limited period those who decided to contract out received an extra 2 per cent rebate above that which the state charged for SERPS.

The Tories' new personal pension was formally introduced in the 1987 Finance Act and came into being on 1 July 1988. It was an immediate hit. The Department of Social Security's working assumption had been that about 500,000 people would take out personal pensions and that the number might ultimately reach 1.75 million. But by the end of April 1990 the take-up was actually 4 million and by 1993–4 had reached 5.7 million. The surge was partly driven by the aggressive sales practices of the main pension providers – the big insurance groups.

Typical of those who bought a personal pension was media professional Noel Harris, from Sevenoaks in Kent, who was 42 at the time. Married with no children, he took out two personal plans with Scottish Life in 1989. The main fund received contributions of over £200 a month, while the second fund was kick-started by a £3,000 opt-out sum from his SERPS contributions. 'Although retirement was some 20-plus years away,' he recalls, 'I realised that my state pension would be inadequate. So, I had to do something about it. Looking at the options, a personal pension seemed right for me. The sums were manageable. The projections looked good. And it gave me a sense of control. It was empowering.'

The 1980s were heady and ground-breaking days. Personal pensions were seen as a self-confident statement and a 'sexy' part of the new Thatcherite provide-for-yourself world of individual responsibility, market freedom and personal choice. Whereas the state system was inadequate, barely providing a living wage and often needing to be supplemented by a complex series of means-tested benefits, private pensions looked to be the business. Indeed, the prime minister wanted to go further and bring in a much larger compulsory private pension. She told her chancellor that they had such a pension arrangement in Switzerland. 'Yes, Prime Minister,' he replied, 'but in Switzerland everything that is not forbidden is compulsory.' There were shadows on the horizon, though. And one of them took the form of a larger-than-life media tycoon, Robert Maxwell.

CHAPTER 3

From Maxwell to mis-selling

Early on 5 November 1991, the bloated body of millionaire newspaper publisher Robert Maxwell was found in the sea off Tenerife in the Canary Islands. He had apparently fallen overboard from his yacht. At first, media attention focused on the mysterious circumstances of his death. Within days, however, revelations about his business dealings began to circulate.

It emerged that he had built up huge debts and had raided at least £425 million from the pension schemes at his principal quoted companies Mirror Group Newspapers and Maxwell Communications Corporation. A few weeks later his sons Kevin and Ian asked that an administrator be appointed to run the private companies. Department of Trade and Industry investigators were duly called in and their enquiries revealed that Maxwell had actually plundered £460 million from the pension funds. It was the largest fraud in modern British corporate history and its sheer audacity took the public's breath away. It led to a great wringing of hands in financial and political circles, as well as public protests, court hearings and eventual changes in the law.

There had been speculation for many years about Maxwell's heavy indebtedness and his seemingly dishonest business practices. But Maxwell had plenty of money, good lawyers and financial advisers, and threats of costly libel actions caused his potential critics to treat him with caution. The evidence suggests that Maxwell's empire – which as well as publishing and the media included electronics, textiles and even football clubs – was built on debt and deception. He could have borrowed money from the pension funds legally had the loan been approved by the trustees and fully disclosed. But Maxwell chose to take millions without permission to prop up the financial position of his other businesses. In the late 1980s he bought and sold companies at a rapid rate, apparently to conceal the unsound foundations of his business.

By 1990 events were starting to catch up with Maxwell, with investigative journalists exploring his manipulation of his companies' pension schemes. In the course of May 1991 it was reported that Maxwell companies and pension schemes were failing to meet statutory reporting obligations. Employees lodged complaints with British and US regulatory agencies about the abuse of company pension funds. As he flew to Gibraltar for that ill-fated final cruise on his yacht, the *Lady Ghislaine*, Maxwell may well have realised that the game was up and that the appalling truth about his questionable practices was about to be made public.

The effect of his fraudulent activities on his employees was devastating. Thousands suddenly found themselves facing an uncertain old age. A typical case was Dennis Stroud and his wife Priscilla. Stroud was working in the finance department of a printing firm in Aldershot, Hampshire during the late 1970s when a distant deal brought the company into the Maxwell orbit. A few years later the firm was shut down and, at 60, he was forced to retire with a lump sum of just £5,000. The former accountant had no idea that his pension had been used to bankroll the controversial publisher's increasingly desperate attempts to stay in business. As the hole in the company pension funds emerged, Stroud discovered that his pension would be less than half that expected. The crucial payments in the final five years of his working life, when he was putting more away in anticipation, had been totally wiped out by the Maxwell fraud.

'When Maxwell died,' Stroud told the *Independent on Sunday* in April 2001, 'I thought, "Good riddance." He was the rudest man I ever came across.' But then came the revelations, and Stroud went on to describe how, frail and on medication for his nerves, he found himself joining protestors waving a placard in the streets outside the Commons. 'I don't know how much money I have lost,' he said. 'It would be too depressing to add up. I am bitter about it. It makes my blood boil.'

How did Maxwell get away with it for so long? After all, his reputation up until the moment he died had not exactly been untarnished. Two decades earlier in 1971 a DTI investigation had concluded that Maxwell was unfit 'to exercise stewardship of a publicly-quoted company'. This did not prevent his return to the stock market as chairman and leading shareholder in not one but two quoted companies. Even so, accountants should have known in the 1980s that the tycoon was using pension fund investments as collateral for takeover bids and that he was moving assets around his empire.

The fact is that whatever warning signals there may have been, Maxwell remained in charge not only of major companies but of the pensions of thousands of people. The root of the problem was the unfettered power he enjoyed as chairman. He was a bully and no one around him was willing to question his actions. His investment banking advisers, including Goldman Sachs, did not stop him from engaging in what would come to be seen as unethical dealings. Quite simply, no one was prepared to stand up to him.

One of the tragedies about the havoc Maxwell wreaked is that the damage, if it could not have been totally prevented, should certainly have been limited. After all, Maxwell was not an isolated occurrence. In March 1991, a few months before his death, inspectors looking in to a similar pension fund fraud involving £1 million at mini-conglomerate Bestwood passed their recommendations to the DTI. These were not immediately published as the Serious Fraud Office was still investigating the company, ultimately obtaining convictions against three people involved in the scandal. However, it should have been possible to pass on those parts of the report not relevant to the SFO inquiry.

The report into Bestwood and its subsidiary Atlanta Fund Managers was written by Gabriel Moss, a leading commercial QC, and John Venning, partner at the accountants Robson Rhodes. Moss and Venning specifically proposed that the level of 'employer-related investment' by pension funds be restricted to five per cent of the fund's assets, that there should be at least one independent trustee on the board of pension funds and that the law be changed so that the funds were managed by someone wholly independent of the employers or trustees. The first and third recommendations, had they been enacted immediately, would have significantly limited what Robert Maxwell was able to do with the pension schemes of his companies. Unfortunately, the DTI did not pass the recommendations in the report to the Department of Social Security until April 1992. Peter Lilley, who was secretary of state for social security at the time of the report, was later called before the Commons Social Security Select Committee to explain the delay.

Maxwell's plundering of company funds clearly raised serious questions about corporate governance and the security of occupational pensions. But while Maxwell was undoubtedly the cause célèbre, dipping into occupational funds was not the preserve of a corrupt few. Other bosses up and down the land were doing the same, arguing that because of fund surpluses – made possible by the stock market boom – they felt at liberty to take 'contribution holidays' and use the money to run and invest in their businesses. Even local councils raided their pension funds at the end of the 1980s to keep poll tax low.

Trustees of such organisations seldom argued with these decisions. By tradition pension trustees were a mix of the professional and the amateur. Many were part-timers and from a non-financial background. Training was encouraged but not mandatory and at this time there was no formal review process of trustee or board performance. So trustees typically lacked the necessary expertise and confidence to check that enough money was actually being paid in, and were often dominated by professional managers, such as the group finance director, seconded from the company. Their dual role as guardians of the pensioners and caretakers of the corporate treasury meant that they had a conflict of interests. As a result they found it increasingly difficult to act always in the very best interests of their millions of members.

Nor did employees – even when aware of what was going on – often object. The 1980s, with the 1986 'Big Bang' in the City – which saw many of the traditional rules governing share dealings swept into the sea – was a period of strong equity markets. Numerous sleepy investments sitting on the books of pension funds soared in value. Contributions continued to flood in. It was a halcyon period of pension fund surpluses. Moreover, company annual reports were not required to record the current health of the pension fund – just the last actuarial valuation – which meant that short-term variations in stock prices had very little effect on the perceived health of the funds. It seemed perverse at the time to undertake annual valuations of funds with liabilities which could stretch ahead for 40 years.

Sadly, the Maxwell affair was not the only scandal to hit the pensions industry in the 1990s. In 1994 it emerged that millions of people who had been persuaded to move from occupational pensions to the new-fangled personal pensions introduced by Margaret Thatcher's government during the late 1980s and early 90s were actually worse off than they would have been if they had stuck with their original scheme. Not only had they lost out on the employers' contributions they would have otherwise received, but the new schemes were inflexible and often incurred steep charges. Nearly two million people were adversely affected in this way.

Much of the blame for the mis-selling of private pensions lay with commission-hungry salesmen dishing out flawed advice. But the government was also at fault. It had given the big pension providers access to public-sector workers like NHS nurses who were then persuaded to swap their 'gold-plated' pensions, accompanied by large NHS employer contributions, for something far more risky. Not only did those involved lose their employer contributions, they also opted for a far less secure form of pension investment, the success of which would be largely dependent on the state of the financial markets in the run-up to retirement.

Adding to the risk was the requirement that they use most of the lump sum accumulated to buy an annuity – a reverse form of insurance which pays out regular sums to the recipient. Annuity rates, however, vary hugely from provider to provider and the returns offered depend on long-term interest rates. An annuity taken out at a time of low inflation and interest rates will deliver far more meagre returns than one taken at a different stage in the economic cycle. It was the promise of guaranteed annuities – higher than normally expected returns – that was to cause Britain's oldest insurer, Equitable Life, to close its doors in December 2000.

An eight-year investigation by the City watchdog the Financial Services Authority (FSA) into the mis-selling scandal (which preceded Equitable Life's collapse) found that £11.8 billion of compensation was eventually paid to those who lost out because of incorrect financial advice. In June 2002 the FSA noted that 1.7 million people had their cases reviewed and received compensation. Disciplinary action had been taken against 346 firms – financial advisers as well as big providers – resulting in fines of £10 million.

As if this were not bad enough, the FSA also discovered that a number of people had been advised to set up a free-standing additional voluntary contribution (FSAVC) because this was deemed to offer tax advantages. In fact, those who were enticed by this would have been far better off making additional voluntary contributions to company schemes since employers often added a generous contribution.

My own employer at the time, the Guardian Media Group, matched every pound paid in by an employee with 50 pence of its own. At the time I was advised by mortgage brokers John Charcol to take out a FSAVC with investment managers M&G, part of the Prudential, as part of a broader mortgage repayment package. When I discovered that I had signed up to an unsuitable scheme M&G

repaid my contributions as well as the extra money I would have earned had I been in the Guardian AVC. Just to add insult to injury it later turned out that the AVC operated for the Guardian was being managed by Equitable Life!

Another typical victim of mis-selling was Brian, who in 1990 contacted financial advisers about saving for his retirement. He was aged 35 at the time and earning £18,000 a year. He was told that he should contract out of SERPS and make regular contributions to a personal pension. As time went by, Brian became increasingly concerned about the arrangements he had agreed to, suspecting that the firm's advice to contract out had been unsuitable. He later asked a claims management company to complain to the firm on his behalf. 'The firm had not considered my attitude to risk or warned me that the value of the pension I would get from the policy was not guaranteed,' he said.

The Maxwell affair rapidly followed by the pensions mis-selling scandal rocked the faith of savers in first occupational pensions and then personal pensions. The body blows to the savings habit were severe. Steps needed to be taken to reassure pensioners and those saving through their companies. The public needed to be protected. Firstly, however, the Maxwell workers had to be looked after. Following a somewhat lengthy battle, a multimillion-pound compensation deal was eventually reached for the majority of the 32,000 victims.

Next, the government acted to try to balance the economy's thirst for strong and dynamic entrepreneurs with the need to ensure publicly quoted companies are run in a professional and trustworthy way. It immediately set about strengthening the latter by asking Sir Adrian Cadbury to chair a committee on the financial aspects of corporate governance. His main reform was an enhanced role for independent non-executive directors, who could put a brake on the activities of an all-too-powerful chairman.

Equally, there was a desperate need to convince the public that the money they were setting aside for their retirement was now being looked after properly. In 1992 Peter Lilley, having left the DTI, in his new role as secretary of state for social security announced that there would be a fundamental review of pension regulation. He set up a committee, under the Oxford don Roy Goode, which would come up with recommendations designed to plug the holes which had allowed the Maxwell scandal to take place.

The Maxwell case showed that a buccaneering entrepreneur could avoid the established network of regulations and controls. One of the main flaws in the system which allowed him to steal from the funds was the failure of the Investment Management Regulatory Organisation (IMRO) to carry out its duties effectively. While the Goode Report in 1994 recommended leaving the regulation of pension fund investment within the control of IMRO (which would be folded into the FSA after Labour came to power in 1997), new safeguards were introduced in 1995 to guard against fraud and incompetence.

The Pensions Act of that year adopted a two-pronged approach. First, it created a watchdog, the Occupational Pensions Regulatory Authority (OPRA), to police the 130,000 occupational pension schemes in Britain – ensuring they were safe and well run. OPRA, which actually came into being in April 1997, was to investigate and take action in claims of 'carelessness or negligence' that might put occupational schemes at risk. In carrying out its duties it had a range of powers, including the ability to fine companies £50,000 and individuals £5,000 and to disqualify fund trustees, who now had to give explicit permission before surpluses could be spent. Second, the government set up an official safety net scheme to ensure that, if the worst happened, people would be compensated properly and promptly, without lengthy battles for a payout. To trigger compensation an employer had to be insolvent and there had to have been a loss. Overseeing this backup insurance for pension funds, paid for by a levy on all occupational schemes, was the Pensions Compensation Board, which sat alongside OPRA. It has to be said, though, that in the four

42

years after these measures were introduced only two payouts were made.

OPRA's own chairman, John Hayes, accepted that 'No system of regulation can positively guarantee things like this will not happen again.' Just four years after the act was introduced a union claimed that British Steel, which later became Corus, was raiding its pension fund to finance a merger with a Dutch firm. The main steelworkers' union said millions of pounds had been transferred from a fund surplus to pay for a merger with Hoogovens to form Europe's largest steel producer. The company rejected claims that it was using pension fund money to finance the merger or give money to shareholders; it said the allegation was a major misinterpretation of the pension fund surplus. 'More than £600 million of the surplus was required to maintain the fund in terms of contributions by the company,' Corus said. 'The company is not giving pension fund money to shareholders and the suggestion that British Steel is dabbling with pension fund money is quite wrong.'

Whatever the rights and wrongs here, there's no doubt that the 1995 legislation was flawed. The government should have required the appointment of an independent custodian for pension schemes and stopped employers playing any role in administering them. That would have removed the temptation to use pension fund assets to support the company. Similarly, the act should have insisted on much greater transparency about the way funds are managed. Instead, the government endorsed the paternalistic culture of occupational pensions, leaving an awful lot up to those running them.

More seriously, the act failed to ring-fence a pension fund's assets in the event of company insolvency. At one point in the drafting of the legislation it was proposed that a clause be introduced to ensure that schemes had sufficient funds to meet their commitments, even if the sponsoring employer went bust. But after strong opposition from some companies, this minimum solvency requirement (MSR) was watered down and its name changed to minimum funding requirement (MFR). Had the MSR standard been adopted, a company's inability to carry on its business would have been picked up earlier and schemes badly damaged by stock market downturns could have been protected. Under the weaker MFR rule, schemes forced into closure had to look after existing pensioners first, with staff not yet retired left to share what remained.

That said, the act did offer some much-needed protection. It stated that pension funds must be able at all times to meet the pension entitlements of members, that some members of the fund had to be appointed as trustees, and that if a fund was rendered insolvent, a levy would be made on the rest of the industry to meet its liabilities.

Perhaps most importantly, the act recognised what the events of the 1990s had manifestly demonstrated: that whichever party was in power, pensions needed to be a major focus of government attention. Unfortunately, when New Labour took power two years later, that lesson was largely forgotten.

CHAPTER 4

At the dawn of New Labour

A pundit asked to comment on the state of British pensions in the lead-up to the 1997 general election would probably have said, 'Well, it's a mixed picture but generally a healthy one.' There were clearly things that needed to be fixed and there were also some major challenges, but there also much that was going right.

On the plus side, the huge swathe of occupational pensions looked to be fairly healthy. Indeed Frank Field, Tony Blair's first minister for pensions, went as far as to say that when Labour gained power in 1997 Britain's occupational pensions were the envy of the world. In the 2004 first Pensions Commission report, Lord Adair Turner noted:

> The UK has had one of the most extensive voluntary funded pensions systems in the world with a higher percentage of people in the occupational schemes, mostly defined benefit in nature, and large pension fund assets as a proportion of GDP.

In the UK pension fund assets represented just over 80 per cent of national output in 2003, against less than 20 per cent in Germany and 5 per cent in France. Only the Netherlands, where several of the biggest employers including Royal Dutch Shell, Unilever, Corus and Reed Elsevier are Anglo-Dutch, boasted a higher number.

Occupational pensions had much to recommend them. From a government point of view, the more people who enrolled in them, the less they would be reliant on state benefits. From an economic point of view, the tens of billions of pounds saved within occupational pensions could be used to fund the requirements of industry, which was normally able to tap the equity-share markets for new funds. From the point of view of the individual, a pension calculated on the salary he or she was earning at the point of retirement was very attractive and could very readily finance years of future activity and enjoyment. And from the point of view of the company, there appeared to be a virtuous circle: when contributions were halted profits went up and shares rose, which boosted the stock market and so benefited pension funds investing in those shares. In 1979 the average company contribution to pension schemes had been 11 per cent of their wage bill. By 1991 this figure had halved because trustees and corporations (often overlapping groups) took the view that funding was more than adequate.

Some even started to question the sheer wealth of the pension fund industry. Conservative Chancellor Nigel Lawson was among them. A rotund figure with a shock of dark hair and a fine intellectual mind, he had come to believe companies were putting too much into their pension funds in attempts to artificially reduce their tax bills and he sought to cap the big surpluses which had built up. In his 1988 Budget, Lawson stipulated that no fund could accumulate assets whose value was greater than 5 per cent of its liabilities. As a result, tax revenues rose by £1 billion a year as firms and their employees strove to reduce pension fund surpluses by reducing the scale of their tax-deductible contributions.

A few years later the public finances lurched deeply into the red as a result of a sharp recession partly caused by the need to keep British interest rates high so that Britain could remain within the Exchange Rate Mechanism (ERM), the precursor to the eurozone single currency. Prime Minister John Major's first chancellor, Norman Lamont, himself an advocate of free markets, found himself in the unenviable position of having to introduce the biggest tax-raising Budget of modern times in 1993 to cope with forecast borrowing of £50 billion or 8 per cent of national output. Buried among the raft of revenue-raising measures was a proposal to reduce the value of the tax credit on dividend payments invested in occupational pension funds. At the time it was little noticed and produced only a mild response from the pensions industry. It did bring in some much-needed cash. But it also left the door guarding pension funds slightly ajar. Four years later New Labour Chancellor Gordon Brown would come blundering through it. On the whole, though, and despite Norman Lamont's actions, company pension funds seemed in robust health.

But there was a challenge on the horizon. The fact is that, however rosy things may look at any given moment, the future stability or otherwise of any pension fund depends on extremely complicated, finely tuned actuarial calculations. In particular, judgements have to be made about the average life expectancy of the scheme's participants. If these turn out to be even slightly out of kilter, then there is a danger that the scheme will run out of cash.

As the 1980s and 90s wore on it became clear that Britons were living longer. In the UK a man who turned 60 in 1981 could expect to live another 16 years and a woman almost 21 years. By 2003 this had increased to 20 years for men and 23 for women, and according to official UK projections by 2026 this will rise to almost 24 years for men and almost 27 for women. Put more bluntly, back in the 1950s an employee lived, on average, only three or four years after retiring at 65. By contrast, a man starting a pension plan in, say, the mid-1980s with a view to retiring at 65, could expect to die at the age of 75 in 2024 – so living on his pension for a full ten years. When the figures were re-examined in 2004 it was found that life expectancy had risen by at least a further four years.

Even these projections could be an underestimate. Actuaries' charts show life-expectancy projections curving to a plateau to match the notion of a biological 'maximum age' beyond which the human race cannot go. But this theory is being challenged by research which suggests that life expectancy may continue to improve in a straight line, as it has done in the past. Catering for this ever-shifting situation has become so tricky for Whitehall to deal with that in October 2005 the government actuary, Chris Daykin, announced that he had stopped assuming that the length of life had some ultimate biological limit. Pensions Regulator Chairman David Norgrove told me in 2009:

It has always been assumed that the rate of increase [in longevity] is going to tail off at some time in the not too distant future. It hasn't and is showing no signs of tailing off. To assume longevity is going to stop growing, as it has in the past, is going against all experience.

In other words, the age we live to could possibly carry on increasing almost indefinitely.

An indication of just how far adrift calcuations were starting to go in the last quarter of the twentieth century was given in the Turner Report of 2005. 'The GAD [Government Actuaries Department],' it stated, 'on the best analysis it could do in 1980, estimated that the life expectancy of a 65-year-old man in 2004 would be a further 14.8 years – and that was the advice going to defined benefit funds at the time. The present estimate is 19 years. So, we got it wrong by about a third.'

In tandem with rising life expectancy in the decades after the Second World War has been a fall in the birth rate. It has been calculated that by 2025 the number of over-60s in Britain will have passed the number of under-25s for the first time. This has huge implications for pensions. In 1999 the working population amounted to 47.8 per cent of the total UK population. By 2030 it will be 44.7 per cent – a potential shortfall of two million workers. One hundred years ago when state pensions were introduced there were 22 people working for every retired person; more recently that figure fell to four; and from 2020 the ratio will be 2:1. Some economists have said that if this silver tsunami continues, instead of having a pyramid of support with myriad workers at its base, each pensioner will rest upon one straining individual, a lonely column of dependency.

Like all alarmist interpretations, this can be accused of being simplistic. It focuses too narrowly on the proportion of older and elderly people in a population, ignoring dependent children and other economically inactive groups, such as women who have left work to bring up families. In fact, at the end of 2008 one in five people were economically inactive in the UK. Just as significantly it makes the wholly wrong assumption that all elderly people are dependent on the rest of society. Nothing could be further from the truth. Many are working longer, others are making a huge contribution to the voluntary sector, and through 'grey' consumption of everything from Saga holidays to medical services older people are making big contributions to national output and the living standards of the whole of society.

Nevertheless, the demographic time bomb undoubtedly poses difficult options. Broadly speaking, Britain, along with other industrialised countries, faces some stark choices: increase the workforce by birth or immigration (as has happened over the last ten years), increase national productivity, or delay retirement significantly. As things are at present, the number of dependent older people in England is projected to grow from 2.5 million in 2001 to just over four million in 2031 – an increase of 57 per cent.

For a while the prospect of fewer people of working age supporting every pensioner was not necessarily seen as a problem. Near-retirees planned to live comfortably off robust pensions and equity released from their homes, which were gaining in value every year. But long-term forecasting is a perilous exercise. In much the same way as population forecasters often get it wrong and mortality predictions have been vulnerable to change, so the country's economy can prove volatile, as the traumatic economic events of 2007–9 – the credit crunch followed by the 'great recession' –

demonstrated only too clearly. Boom does give way to bust. When this happens, it wreaks havoc with people's savings in whatever form they are kept – from buy-to-let to conventional savings.

No policymaker has a crystal ball, but it should have been clear to everyone in the lead-up to the 1997 general election that pensions were going to be a major issue in the years ahead. Occupational pensions seemed astonishingly healthy but, just as with the state pension, the challenge was to keep them vigorous in an era of growing life expectancy and therefore greater calls on the funds available. As the Maxwell scandal and the debacle surrounding the mis-selling of personal pensions showed, there was also a need for close and continuing scrutiny.

Furthermore, occupational pensions had become an ever more important component of the nation's welfare system for old age, taken up by an increasing number of people at a time when the state pension had been effectively cut back by the Thatcher government's decision to remove the link between the annual rise in the universal state pension and the annual rise in earnings. They needed to be protected. Labour MP Frank Field went so far as to describe the increasing emphasis the Tories placed on occupational and personal pensions as their 'major welfare innovation'.

One consequence of the British approach to pensions was that they became – and continue to be – much less of a burden on the state than has been the case in many other countries. Countries in the EU have traditionally regarded large tax increases and social security contributions as necessary to fund future liabilities.

In Germany state pensions consumed 11.8 per cent of gross domestic product in 2000 and are forecast to rise to 16.9 per cent by 2050. In contrast Britain's state pensions system absorbs just 5.5 per cent of GDP, a figure which the European Policy Committee of the EU projects will fall to 4.4 per cent by 2050 if there are no policy changes. Britain, along with Ireland, New Zealand and Canada, views the state pension as a safety net to prevent poverty rather than an income replacement mechanism which comes into play on retirement. It's no wonder, therefore, that so many recipients regarded it as inadequate.

The Conservatives themselves were aware that further work on pensions was needed. Over the summer of 1996, just 12 months before the next general election, the Major government embarked on a third stage of reform. The then secretary of state for social security, Peter Lilley, began work on new proposals to deal with the problem of the perceived inadequate provision. His Basic Pension Plus plans – which never saw the light of day – proposed that the basic state pension and SERPS would be replaced with a state guarantee.

On 1 May 1997 a weary and beleaguered Conservative government under John Major was heavily defeated by a newly energised Labour Party under Tony Blair. Pensions should have been high on the new government's agenda; they were, after all, an issue that would at some point or other directly affect just about everyone in the country. What's more there were clearly problems and policy questions that needed to be addressed.

Labour should have been well-suited for the task ahead. A party with a history of welfare reform, carried to power on a wave of popular euphoria, they also had the Commons majority to allow them to think boldly. And they had inherited a booming economy that would allow them to put ambitious plans into action. New Labour were in an excellent position to make pensions fit for purpose in the new millennium on the horizon.

What followed was a shambles.

PART TWO

Betraying

CHAPTER 5

Gordon's smash and grab

The day after the 1997 election the new chancellor Gordon Brown arrived at the grand portals of the Treasury on Great George Street. He was accompanied by the Hotel Group, the coterie of advisers he had surrounded himself with in the build-up to the election victory. Among them were the gregarious businessman-turned-politician Geoffrey Robinson, now paymaster general, and the political bruiser Charlie Whelan, now his spokesman. 'It's a sad day,' muttered one Treasury mandarin. 'We've never previously allowed spivs to set foot inside this building.'

Officials felt a sense of unease, and this was not helped by what followed. On arrival, according to Brown's biographer Tom Bower, Brown's team watched a presentation about the economy. Historically, in Britain such briefings for incoming chancellors have been painful affairs with dire predictions – of crisis in the public finances, runaway inflation and an impending sterling crisis. But Brown's legacy from his Conservative predecessor Ken Clarke was surprisingly robust. 'These are fantastically good figures,' said an official, describing Labour's inheritance from the Tories. 'The state of the economy is much better than predicted.' 'What am I meant to do with this?' Brown reportedly snarled. 'Write a thank-you letter?' This off-handed sarcasm set the tone for Brown's frosty relations with the most senior of his Treasury officials.

Brown had not been idle as Labour prepared for government and knew precisely what he wanted to do in the mini-Budget that traditionally follows the arrival of a new chancellor at Number 11. He knew that unless the initiative is seized early on, inertia can all too easily set in. Not only was he preparing for radical reforms to the economy – most notably creating an independent Bank of England – he was determined to make the Treasury the power house for Labour's domestic policy, dominant over all other departments and as independent of Number 10 as was politically feasible. It would be his base for challenging Tony Blair and preparing his own leadership ambitions.

Among the controversial blueprints in Brown's box of tricks was the plan, prepared by accountants from Arthur Andersen, to remove the tax credit which pension funds received on dividend payments from companies in which they were invested. The highly sensitive proposal had been tucked away in the safe in Robinson's penthouse suite at the Grosvenor House Hotel until it was unleashed on a startled Whitehall. Brown argued that the credit harmed the economy by encouraging firms to pay big dividends to shareholders rather than re-invest in their business. He pointed to the fact that Norman Lamont and the Conservatives had already trimmed the relief in 1993. Just as importantly, he argued, company pension funds were in surplus and could handle the change.

The Treasury began an urgent and detailed assessment of the plan, looking at every possible angle. Unfortunately for Brown and his group, many of the professional economists' findings differed from those arrived at by the accountants Andersen and Brown's cohorts, although it has to be said that Andersen themselves had expressed reservations. In the months running up to the 1997 election Andersen had quietly road tested the ideas with leading City figures such as (Sir) Peter Davies, then chief executive of the mighty Prudential insurance group. After the dividend tax credit was axed, action was taken to prevent the facts from being made public for several years. It was only after a campaign by the national newspapers, with *The Times* in the forefront, that he was eventually forced to relent, and the details were revealed in 2007 following an appeal under the Freedom of Information Act. Ironically, this act had been introduced by New Labour early in its first term of office as part of its commitment to more open government.

What has now emerged is that Brown commissioned some of the best brains in the Treasury and Inland Revenue to tell him what the potential implications might be. He then received four Treasury papers. Each conceded a degree of uncertainty about its predictions, but all disagreed with what was proposed.

The papers outlined a range of scenarios, but the common thread was that each argued that the value of pension funds would fall. One paper was particularly prescient given what eventually happened, predicting a drop of up to £75 billion in the value of private pension plans. It feared that the Brown plan would be particularly hard on the eight million in private pension schemes and the self-employed. In addition, it forecast that 'employers would have to contribute about an extra £10 billion a year for the next 10 to 15 years to get pension scheme funding back on track'.

Another of the documents, drawn up by the Inland Revenue, concluded that 'abolishing tax credits would make a big hole in pension scheme finances'. Pension schemes would need an extra £3 billion to £4 billion a year to meet their commitments and future pension benefits would suffer.

Brown was also warned that the changes would encourage firms to end final salary schemes, by which pensioners receive a fixed proportion of their salary at retirement. 'The present shift towards defined contribution schemes might accelerate,' the documents stated.

Employees would have to increase contributions if pensions were to be maintained. In practice, we would expect contributions to be increased only by those people who could afford to pay more. The change would therefore lead to a reduction in pension benefits to the lower-paid.

It looked as though Brown and his cohorts were not only planning to attack corporate benefits they regarded as being too generous to companies, they were also prepared to hit their own core voters – ordinary low-paid workers who had committed years to their sometimes less than stimulating jobs in the belief that a comfortable retirement was ahead of them.

The Inland Revenue warned that someone on an average company pension of £5,000 a year could lose anything between £150 and £1,000 a year. 'Quite clearly,' it said, 'any loss of pension could be difficult for someone with a small income to cope with.' It also warned that 'everyone in a money purchase scheme is a potential loser'. This was a key point. In those companies where the expense of gold-plated final salary schemes had become too great, employees had been persuaded to switch into less attractive defined con-tribution, or money purchase, schemes where returns were directly related to the performance of financial markets. It followed that if the dividend income were cut by the government, overall returns on stock market investment would diminish along with prospective pensions.

The submissions to Brown were made in May and June 1997, ahead of the July Budget. At their bleakest they predicted a stock market fall of between 6 and 20 per cent, a cost of billions of pounds to savers and a possible public backlash. It is not clear from the documents whether officials actually advised that the policy be scrapped, but there is absolutely no doubt that they believed Brown was playing roulette with Britain's system of occupational and private pensions, one of the most admired in Europe. The precise policy recommendations at the time have been kept secret. Only one piece of advice – that the change should have been phased in – was published. That advice, like all the other cautions in the Treasury papers, was ignored.

Brown and his advisers were so hooked on the idea that occupational pensions were too generous to corporate Britain they did not seem to recognise that if the system was weakened the burden, as in continental Europe, would fall back on the state. They were determined to go ahead with what had finally been decided at the Grosvenor House Hotel. Brown's final decision rested on several lines of argument. Firstly, he believed that dividend tax credits harmed the economy by encouraging firms to pay big dividends rather than re-invest in their business. Secondly, he pointed out that company pension funds were in surplus and taking lengthy pension holidays, and could afford the change. Thirdly, he argued that the Conservatives had spotted the dangers of British companies paying bigger dividends than their continental rivals and had already nibbled away at the credit – most notably when Norman Lamont cut it to 20 per cent in 1993. Finally, he noted that the Treasury papers conceded that a buoyant stock market – at the time rising by an average of 15 per cent a year – could mitigate any potential loss caused by the abolition of the pension tax credit.

Brown's team sought to sell the reform as a long-overdue modernisation and streamlining of the corporate tax system. This was how it was presented in the July 1997 Budget speech. In the first of nearly 20 such appearances at the dispatch box, Brown told a packed Commons that he was cutting the top rate of Corporation Tax from 33 per cent to 31 per cent, 'the lowest rate ever in the UK'. He continued:

This tax is the first component of this Budget's investment strategy. The second is a structural reform that will also encourage investment. The present system of tax credits encourages companies to pay out dividends rather than reinvest their profits. This cannot be the best way of encouraging investment for the long term as was acknowledged by the last government.

Many pension funds are in substantial surplus at present and many companies are enjoying pension holidays, so this is the right time to undertake long needed reform. So with immediate effect, I propose to abolish tax credits paid to pension funds and companies.

The speech gloss hid the real agenda here. In his memoirs Geoffrey Robinson states that Brown's driving factors were his need to put money in the Treasury coffers and his desire to eliminate what he perceived as a 'structural deficit' in the public finances. 'The corporate sector would have to bear the brunt of the inescapable necessity to raise taxes. That was our starting point and we set a target of increasing revenues by £5 billion per annum,' Robinson states in his memoir *The Unconventional Minister*, published in 2000. During a conversation with me in his cluttered Portcullis House office in Westminster in 2009 Robinson went further:

> The driving motives were, if you bottom line on it, we were seeking to raise money . . . We needed it; behind the great blather, we simply hadn't broken the back of the deficit.

Brown's first Budget contained several headline-making decisions. The Bank of England was to be made independent. A windfall tax was to be levied on the privatised utilities – a popular move given the controversy over the pay and bonuses received by bosses of the former state companies, most notably the unfortunate chief executive of British Gas, Cedric Brown. Corporation Tax was to be cut. With all of this going on, and the change in the tax relief on dividends buried in technicalities, there was clearly a belief among Brown and his team that one of the landmark changes of Labour's years in office could be smuggled into the Finance Act without creating negative publicity.

Mike Warburton, the public face of accountants Grant Thornton – later on one of the expert witnesses in the legal battle to get the Treasury documents released – recalled:

> The government was warned but they seemed more concerned that people in the industry would complain. This was a tightly made decision by a tight cluster of people, without proper regard for the huge number of people in this country saving for

their retirement. In financial terms, there is nothing more important than saving for retirement. To introduce such a measure without proper debate is extraordinary and totally unacceptable. All they were worried about was being able to announce the Budget and get away with it.

That said, the plans did get one semi-public airing before the Budget. Amid the greatest secrecy, the Brown team road tested their ideas with the accountants Andersen in a project codenamed Cascade. I was at that time financial editor of the *Guardian*, and came to hear of this in the weeks leading up to the May 1997 election. However, I was faced with such forceful denials at the time that I felt I could not run the story.

It's perhaps not surprising that Brown's plans were hatched and tested in extraordinary secrecy. What is astonishing is that it seems possible that even Prime Minister Tony Blair was among those kept in the dark. It was an early sign both of Brown's determination to keep a distance between himself and the Number 10 machine and of the political split that would mark Blair's relationship with Brown in the decade they were to share at the heart of the New Labour government. The fracture almost certainly went back to the mid-1990s, when Blair jumped ahead of Brown in the race to become Labour leader after John Smith's death. The schism could often be seen in Cabinet, where the argumentative Brown would push to have his way on domestic issues even when the PM demurred.

Even at the point that Blair was made aware of the proposal, he seems not to have known that officials had their doubts. When a civil servant then warned him that the costs of Brown's plans could be 'enormous' and the consequences 'unsolvable', he did not take action. The official later reported, 'The Prime Minister was reluctant to engage the Chancellor.' Derek Scott, Blair's Downing Street economic adviser at the time, also believes that while the PM should have challenged Brown on the tax raid, he chose not to. 'I doubt very much he was given the full picture or warnings,' he said.

It was a hell of a job to get anything out of the Treasury even at that time. It was presented to Number 10 as a way of removing a tax distortion and the effects wouldn't matter as the stock market was pretty buoyant. But it was a mad thing to do. There was a half-hour discussion about it at the time, but Blair was clearly not prepared to take it on.

The forceful Brown was a hard man to resist and strongly opposed to any voices that dissented from his own. In a *Financial Times* article in March 2007 Lord Turnbull, former permanent secretary to the Treasury, referred to Brown's alleged 'Stalinist ruthlessness'. He said of Brown's relationship with his colleagues:

He cannot allow them any serious discussion about priorities. His view is that it is just not worth it, and "they will get what I decide". And that is an extremely insulting kind of process.

Here, then, were the wrangles and secretive goings-on in Whitehall that formed the backdrop to Budget Day, 2 July. Early that afternoon, Brown – complete with his new scarlet leather Budget box, made of yellow pine with a brass handle and lock in his Fife constituency – was whisked in the ministerial Rover from the Treasury across Parliament Square. Such was the wall of secrecy that had surrounded the pension issues that few immediately grasped the significance of what was being announced. As the Tory MP and later shadow chancellor George Osborne later recalled:

Of course, when Labour members listened to the chancellor make his Budget speech at the Dispatch Box, they could not have guessed that when he promised to undertake a long-needed reform of company taxation to encourage investment, he meant that he was about to clobber their pensions with a stealth tax worth £5 billion a year.

When the inevitable criticism was voiced, New Labour argued that tinkering with dividend tax credits was nothing new. They pointed to the fact that the Conservatives had been there before them – on five occasions over 18 years – most notably when Nigel Lawson taxed surpluses on pension funds and his successor Norman Lamont cut dividend tax credits in 1993 because they distorted the market. Documents released by the Treasury in July 2007 show that Lamont was advised by civil servants that £1 billion a year could be raised by reducing dividend tax credits from 25 per cent to 20 per cent.

The Tories countered by saying that, unlike Brown, Lamont had never planned to use the revenue gained to cut corporation or capital gains tax. There was also a big difference between taxing surpluses or reducing the level of tax credits, and outright abolition. When it was suggested to Lamont's successor Kenneth Clarke that he might consider such a radical approach, he demurred, knowing what damage it might cause.

The City and investment community were muted in their response, in part because the implications of the move took a while to absorb, in part because they were unwilling to make an enemy of a new chancellor just finding his way. The press, right and left, was too enthralled with the reforming zeal of the new regime after 17 years of Conservative rule to make a serious issue of such a recherché matter as retirement provision, which was difficult to understand and explain. The complex concepts involved – advanced corporation tax and dividend income, for example – were unpromising material for headlines.

Specialists, however, quickly grasped what was going on. The industry body for private sector pensions, the National Association of Pension Funds (NAPF), was horrified. Its chairman Peter Murray condemned the move as the 'biggest attack on pension provision since the war'. It estimated that it would require employers to contribute an extra £50 billion to pension funds over the next decade. 'Even Robert Maxwell took only £400 million,' Murray argued.

It was not long before the risks of Brown's strategy became apparent, and pensions started to come under pressure. Much of the chancellor's strategy was predicated on the dangerous belief that the economy would continue to improve. 'We will not put hard-won economic stability at risk,' he said in a speech at the 2000 Labour conference. 'No return to short-termism. No return to Tory boom and bust.' Inevitably, though, the economy did from time to time hit choppy waters. Shares did not tumble immediately in the wake of Brown's 1997 Budget, but in 2000, four years after the former Federal Reserve chairman Alan Greenspan had warned of 'irrational exuberance' in stock markets, shares plummeted as the bubble in technology shares burst. Greenspan's warning that equity prices had climbed too high had been ignored by the Labour government in 1997 and by investors infected by a herd instinct to be part of the boom. Prudent governments listen to such warnings and change their behaviour accordingly, but Brown gambled that the bull market in shares was to stay. Seven years later an even more serious economic crisis, initially put in train by the collapse of the sub-prime mortgage market in the US, swept the world, and Britain faced recession.

A December 2009 study by investment bankers Morgan Stanley established that the noughties (the years 2000 to 2010) represented the worst period for shares on the London Stock Exchange since the Great Crash of 1929. The total return for investors fell by 1.8 per cent a year throughout the decade. The insane belief that share prices always rise (because they had in the recent past), which contributed to Brown and Balls ignoring Treasury advice in 1997, was revealed to be an appalling misjudgment.

Had it not been for that fateful decision in Brown's first Budget, pension funds might well have been able to weather these storms. But the reality was that they were not equipped to absorb the loss of £5 billion to £6 billion a year in tax-free dividend income. This was not just a straight loss each year. When I joined Sir James Crosby, an actuary and the former chief executive of Halifax Bank of Scotland, in his Bishopsgate office in the City for lunch in 2005 he did a quick back-of-the-serviette calculation to look at how much future value (using a discounted cash flow model) had been lost by the abolition of the tax credit.

He calculated the loss of income to be in the order of a staggering £100 billion – sufficient, in other words, to meet the challenges facing the pensions industry: longer life expectancy, the cost of increased regulation, the weak stock market, all could have been absorbed. Crosby's figure was an underestimate. In January 2009 the Office of National Statistics (ONS) calculated that the black hole in defined benefit pension schemes – the pride of Britain's occupational system – had reached an astonishing £194.5 billion. The thoroughly spurious claims by Brown and those around him that corporate funds were rich enough to take the punishment proved to be complacent in the extreme. In a mere ten years New Labour had reduced almost a century of secure retirement to rubble.

Part of the problem was that the removal of the tax credit also did irreparable damage to the stock market by making shares less attractive to hold for pension funds and the life insurance companies which run private pension plans. A report on pension trends published by the ONS in January 2010 found that as a proportion of gross domestic product – the nation's total output – the value of assets in life assurance and pension funds was below the 1999 peak of 176 per cent. In 2008 the value of these funds had fallen to £1.8 trillion or just 128 per cent of GDP.

The 1997 dividend tax heist had turned the nation's previously wealthy private-sector occupational pensions system into a basket case and a headache for almost every company in Britain, including the richest and most profitable like oil giant BP. But worse, it tore the underpinnings from stock market investment, diminishing returns and decimating the nation's savings. Brown's ill-conceived policy – implemented against best advice and without proper consultation – proved a disaster. It was a far more important factor in the ruination of the nation's pension system than the imposition of tighter regulation and changes in mortality assumptions. There is good reason to believe that had the dividend tax credit remained intact the retirement crisis – which Britain now faces – would never have happened.

In the public sector, where several pension funds were invested in the stock market, local authorities were hard hit. In 2006 Chancellor Brown was warned that the local government pension scheme, with 1.3 million members, would require extra contributions. By now more than a quarter of the revenue raised by council tax bills was going towards pension payments rather than ensuring that the roads were repaired and the bins emptied. The Treasury had feared a 'reduction in pension benefits for the lower paid'. Now it was happening. The government would be forced to increase the Pension Credit – a form of means testing – for those on low incomes who could no longer rely on occupational pensions for a decent living standard.

But the biggest impact was felt by final salary schemes in the private sector. In these plans employers effectively shoulder investment risks because they guarantee the benefits – if investments don't keep up with commitments, a black hole can open very rapidly. At the end of 2009 the pension experts Aon Consulting reported that the black hole in the top 200 gold-plated final salary pension plans had soared to £100 billion. Employers had been told by government that they might have to fork out additional contributions, but the sums required to keep schemes solvent were soaring and major companies were estimated to be paying in at least £5 billion a year extra to cut pension deficits.

In 2002 I received a note from an employee of the leading audit firm Ernst & Young. It contained a letter from the firm peremptorily informing the 2,000 members of the £410 million final salary pension scheme that it was being closed and they would be transferred into a money purchase scheme. It was a precedent-setting break in a pension commitment to an existing workforce, and all the more surprising in that those making the decision belonged to a professional firm that might have been expected to have placed commitment to its workforce above all else. The move was challenged by the employers concerned and more generous compensation was agreed that provided for the loss of the scheme. But the Rubicon had been crossed. Final salary schemes for existing members were no longer sacrosanct.

Shortly afterwards a similar missive from the struggling food retailer Iceland revealed that its new management, headed by company rescue specialist Bill Grimsey, was planning the same thing. In a letter to employees of the publicly quoted enterprise Grimsey said, 'These old final salary arrangements are expensive to maintain, unpredictable in terms of costs, and currently absorb one-quarter of the group's profits.' As a result the scheme would be closed to 4,400 workers, who would be shifted to a money purchase scheme.

The disclosure of this action harmed Grimsey's reputation as a friend to the ordinary workers of the companies in which he was involved. I criticised him in my *Daily Mail* column, and in a face-to-face meeting we then had over breakfast in the elegant surroundings of the Goring Hotel, just off Buckingham Palace Road in central London, hard words were exchanged. The fact was that he was the first known chief executive to abrogate a final salary pension scheme. Criticism rained down on him from all sides. Actuaries Lane Clark & Peacock described the move as 'radical and a departure from the norm'. The Transport and General Workers Union charged that the workers in the final salary scheme were being punished as a 'direct result of existing management' and said the result would be 'a demotivated workforce'.

By now the trend of closures was becoming unmistakeable. In March 2004 the *Financial Times* reported that most of Britain's 100 biggest companies could shut their final salary pension schemes to existing workers as well as new members within six years. A review of the UK pensions market by Lane Clark & Peacock showed that in 2003–4, some 92 of the FTSE 100 companies had a final salary scheme that was now closed to new members. Many companies had only just stopped short of closing them to existing employees, fearing the anger it would cause. But it was only a matter of time before this practice became widespread.

The precedent set by Ernst & Young would open the floodgates for other companies to do the same thing. In 2005 Rentokil Initial, the royal rat-catcher and cleaning services firm, became the first FTSE 100 company to shut its final salary scheme to existing employees. Early in 2006 it was joined by the department store group Harrods, which closed its scheme to 1,500 people. Another publicly quoted retailer, Debenhams, up to its neck in debt as a result of a buyout by private equity, closed its defined benefits scheme to existing workers in August 2006, again citing stock market volatility.

In January 2010 Alliance Boots, owners of Boots the Chemist, revealed it was closing its final salary pension scheme to some 15,000 employees who had been paying into the plan for decades. This was despite the fact that the Boots scheme had been one of the first to take defensive action, after the Brown tax raid, by reinvesting its portfolio in government stocks to protect itself from future stock market unpredictability. The worry about stock market turbulence, it need hardly be repeated, was one of the main reasons why Gordon Brown had been counselled against abolishing the dividend tax credit almost a decade earlier.

Most of the firms that cancelled their final salary pension plans moved future retirees into money purchase schemes. In effect they were shifting the risk of running retirement plans from employers and their shareholders to employees, replacing a robust pensions system with one that was far less durable. Aon Consulting, the human resources adviser, warned that even these were in danger from government policy. Aon director Donald Duval argued that regulation would reduce the flexibility of such schemes. He was concerned the government might attempt to interfere with the level of contributions employers made, or even force them to make guarantees.

By 2008 Aon was reporting that final salary schemes were nearly dead. One scheme after another had closed or seen its benefits diluted for members, and much of the blame was heaped on Brown's tax changes. An Aon survey of over 100 pension scheme managers revealed that the number of schemes open to new members now stood at a record low, with 83 per cent of such schemes having closed to new members in recent years.

Two of the biggest blows would come in the wake of the credit crunch of 2007–9. For decades British Petroleum, the nation's richest company, had boasted one of the UK's best occupational pension plans. Its largely non-contributory final salary plan covered more than 69,000 people, some 39,000 of whom were at that time drawing their pensions. In June 2009 it revealed that from April 2010 the final salary plan would be axed and new employees would pay between 5 per cent and 15 per cent of their salaries into a new money purchase scheme. The move came despite the fact that the BP scheme had a surplus of almost £1 billion at the end of its 2008 financial year and labour costs were a mere fraction of the group's total expenses bill.

Within 24 hours of the BP secession from final salary pensions there was another devastating blow. Barclays, one of the survivors of the credit crunch and ensuing great panic, announced that it was going one step further than BP. It had already closed its scheme to new entrants in 1997, transferring workers into a plan directly dependent on stock market returns. Now it was closing its final salary pension scheme to existing members. Some 18,000 workers would be affected. In a letter to employees the bank's chief executive John Varley noted that the scheme, which had had a surplus of £200 million in September 2008, had moved into a deficit of £2.2 billion a year later. He said that these were huge numbers in the context of the group's stock market value and profit and loss account. Rob MacGregor of the Unite union expressed outrage at the bank's behaviour. 'The attack on pensions for the loyal and hard-working staff at the bank is utterly alarming.'

The one major UK employer to leave its final salary scheme intact for all its workers was the global grocery giant Tesco. The group's chief executive Sir Terry Leahy regards the pension scheme as an essential part of the grocer's compensation package. In 2009 Leahy told me he saw the pension plan as a means of building loyalty among a workforce which, in the broader scheme of things, was comparatively low paid. Even though the scheme, now the largest in the UK, was in deficit, Leahy said he was committed to keep it open.

For some companies problematic pension funds had, in the course of the noughties, become the tail wagging the dog. Among the companies struggling with vast legacy deficits were the nation's flag carrier British Airways, British Telecom and the government-owned Royal Mail. Far from improving the financial situation of British industry and encouraging new investment, as Brown and his colleagues had claimed would happen, plugging the holes in occupational pensions was starting to take priority over all else.

The depressing statistics speak for themselves. In 1995, before the pensions tax credit was removed, according to data produced by the Office of National Statistics there were nearly five million people in open final salary pension schemes. By start of the new millennium this number had fallen to just over four million. At the end of 2008 the number had shrunk to less than one million. Even these numbers don't quite reveal the full scale of the decline. As a result of a curious bit of accounting in the year 2000 the government reclassified two large public-sector bodies – the Post Office and the BBC, both with big defined benefit schemes – to the private sector. Perhaps the easiest way to appreciate what has happened is to look at two simple figures. In 1997, 90 per cent of private-sector occupational pensions were final salary. A decade later, two-thirds of these had been closed to new members.

Because pensions seem so technical, it can be difficult to appreciate what a switch from one type to another actually means in practical terms. This has been exacerbated by the tendency of employers and pension plans to refer to the new schemes being brought in as 'defined contribution' – a label that doesn't sound that different from 'defined benefit'.

In fact, everything changes when you move from a final salary, or defined benefit, scheme to a defined contribution one – even leaving aside the consideration that many companies have used the introduction of revised schemes for new employees as an excuse to cut contribution levels. Future pensions will largely depend on the performance of the trustees and their advisers as managers of investment funds. Those people unlucky enough to retire during a downdraft in financial markets will see their expected pensions substantially reduced.

A government requirement that most of the pension pot built up has to be used to buy an annuity, a form of reverse insurance which pays a regular sum for life, means that the choices for people retiring are strictly limited. It also exposes them to another market uncertainty in the shape of the yields (interest rate returns) on government stocks, on which annuity rates are based. In effect, people are left to the tender mercies of two market places – shares and government stocks (gilts) – which can be hard to comprehend and whose stability cannot be guaranteed.

One example will suffice to show just what a change to a person's life a switch in pension can bring about. Andrew Parr of Minster, Kent was a steelworker for Allied Steel & Wire at Sheerness for 20 years. He was made redundant in December 2002, at which point he expected to receive a pension of £15,500 a year. What he actually got was £7,000. In his view:

All the problems with pensions are Gordon Brown's. He took a pension scheme that was the envy of the world and in ten years turned it into a basket case. Actually, he didn't take ten years, he took about a month, but it's taken ten years to spot what he's done. He's an incredibly cynical chancellor. He ignored the advice of his own people.

It was not that long before the full implications of Brown's 1997 raid started to be appreciated and the media began to dig. *The Times* instructed its lawyers to apply for the release of official documents showing what the Treasury's advice had been in the lead-up to Brown's fateful decision. Not surprisingly, the Treasury – with Brown at that stage still at the helm – objected and tried to get the matter kicked into the long grass. The Treasury insisted the documents should remain secret under a clause in the Freedom of Information legislation that states that policy advice does not have to be disclosed.

A two-year stalemate ensued. But the paper was persistent and eventually, in the summer of 2006, its patience paid off when the Information Commissioner ruled against the Treasury and declared that the release of the documents was in the public interest. The Treasury nevertheless continued to prevaricate and stuck to its official line.

Ed Balls, by then an MP and economic secretary at the Treasury, told the BBC Radio Four's *Today* programme in March 2007, 'We decided on the basis of Civil Service advice to go ahead [with the pensions tax hit] because this was the best thing for the long-term investment of the UK economy.' He also stated that in 1996 the Confederation of British Industry (CBI) had suggested to Brown that it would favour the abolition of dividend tax credits, if this was accompanied by a cut in Corporation Tax. Balls claimed the CBI had said to Brown, 'You haven't gone far enough: you have to act in a decisive way in the long-term interests of British companies and British investors.'

Balls' claim of support from the employers' group was immediately rejected by Lord Turner, director general of the CBI at the time the group was alleged to have spoken to Brown. Turner told the BBC, 'Over the years there has been a claim by Ed Balls and Gordon Brown that one member at the CBI Presidents' Committee said he thought it was a good idea . . . I have no record of this.' It was 'definitely not me', he added. 'At no stage was this official policy of the CBI; at no stage did anyone with authority to speak for the CBI say that was our policy. At the 1997 election we expressed doubt – before the Budget.'

As pressure mounted for the release of key documents, the Treasury – possibly fearing what Lord Turnbull (permanent secretary at the Treasury at the time of the tax raid) might say at a new hearing – announced that it was withdrawing the objection to the release of its internal papers. The timing was interesting. Just after the start of the Commons' Easter recess, and with Brown thousands of miles away in Afghanistan, the Treasury posted some documents, without fanfare, on its website late on a Friday afternoon.

If it had been hoping that no one would notice, however, Brown's inner circle were to be disappointed. Several newspapers, including the *Daily Mail*, led their front pages the following day with the news that the chancellor had been warned of the consequences of his 1997 tax raid.

The cat was now out of the bag and the Conservatives immediately called for an independent inquiry by the government actuary. 'The chancellor has effectively concealed information surrounding these plans from Parliament for the past ten years,' said Philip Hammond, shadow work and pensions secretary. 'The chancellor has been telling us for the past ten years that these tax changes didn't have a negative effect on pension funds. The documents now prove this is not true.'

Liberal Democrat Treasury spokesman Vince Cable, a cerebral and widely respected political figure and economist, was blunt about the impact of the pensions tax raid. 'Gordon Brown's desire to increase taxes through the back door, rather than being honest, has resulted in a great deal of damage to private and occupational pension funds,' he said. 'Not only did these tax changes cause great damage . . . but the damage was premeditated.'

As soon as the Commons resumed after the Easter recess, the Tories seized the initiative. Shadow Chancellor George Osborne told

MPs on 17 April that the Treasury's advice was clear. Of Gordon Brown, he said:

The first and worst of his mistakes was that raid on pensions. The plans for the pension tax raid were, strangely enough, dreamt up in a hotel room. They were dreamt up by the small cabal of the then shadow chancellor, which included the economics secretary, in the penthouse suite of the Grosvenor House Hotel taken by the Honourable Member for Coventry North-West [Geoffrey Robinson]. He is the chancellor's former paymaster in more ways than one. It is all there in the Honourable Member's memoirs.

It is clear from the memoirs that right from the start the tax on pensions was never about encouraging retained profits or increased investment, or any of the other excuses that the chancellor still peddles. Mr Robinson says in his book, 'We needed the money. It had to come from somewhere. We set a target of increasing revenues by £5 billion per annum . . . There were not many options. If the target was going to be met, then tax credits had to go.'

The government kept their stealth plans secret – from the public, from the rest of the Labour Party and even from the then leader of the Opposition. Clearly, the chancellor was starting as he meant to continue. According to the Robinson memoirs the tax plans were locked in a safe in that hotel room throughout the election campaign, while the rest of the Labour Party went round the country promising not to increases taxes at all.

For their part, the government denied that Gordon Brown's actions in 1997 could be blamed for what followed. In 2007 one of the architects of the tax change, Ed Balls, explained:

The reason why subsequently we had more pressure in

pensions has been because of the £250 billion fall in the stock markets, plus the evidence that people are living longer, plus the evidence that at that time in 1997 companies were not making the kind of provision which they needed to make, given those pressures.

In December of the same year Mike O'Brien, the minister for pensions reform, claimed in a speech to the City law firm Eversheds that the steady fall in membership of defined benefit pension schemes was caused 'by inescapable long-term trends. Changes in inflation and the stock market bubbles have contributed. But the most important factor is longevity. Since the beginning of the twentieth century we have been revising longevity figures ever upwards.' Everything was to blame, in other words, except New Labour policy.

Others have seen it differently. Economist Ros Altmann, for example, became an outspoken critic of the government as the scale of Labour's betrayal became clear. Altmann argued that the government paid lip service to encouraging pension savings while systematically destroying the incentive to put money away for retirement for most of the population. As she put it:

This chancellor [Gordon Brown] will go down in history as the one who destroyed our pensions system. He just ignores what he doesn't want to hear, then tries to cover up the consequences and hide it from everybody . . . He clearly decided pension funds were a ripe target, but this was completely irresponsible government. It put final salary schemes at risk. They were warned this would happen and the predictions have come true. Brown knowingly destroyed what was once one of the great pension systems in the world and he did it deliberately.

That one fateful change announced in the 1997 Budget has

affected 11 million people with company pensions and a further seven million with personal pensions. It is interesting to note that when Labour came to power one of the greatest concerns about Britain joining euroland was that the UK – which was providing good pensions for almost half its workforce – might end up paying the bill for countries like Germany, which had failed to make provision. Things couldn't be more different now.

And, as subsequent events over the past 13 years have shown, Gordon Brown's 1997 Budget sleight of hand – with all the havoc it would create – is not the only charge that can be made against New Labour's record on pensions.

CHAPTER 6

The compensation cold shoulder

The edgy seaside resort of Brighton, with its exotic mixture of alternative lifestyles, is used to protests and strange sights. But few could compete with a group of middle-aged men stripped entirely naked and sheltering behind a banner demanding justice for their pensions. It was 25 September 2005 and Gordon Brown was about to take to the podium in the Brighton Centre to deliver his annual tub-thumping speech, outlining his vision for Britain as 'a home-owning, share-owning democracy for everyone' and also laying out the vision for his own administration when Tony Blair stepped down.

While Brown talked of a Thatcher-style agenda of giving everyone the chance to control their own economic fate through home ownership and share investment, those shivering outside, surrounded by a melee of press photographers, were claiming that they had been abandoned by Downing Street and Whitehall. This was a very public act of despair by workers who had spent all their lives in the steel industry but had been left high and dry by the chancellor when their firm went bust, taking their hard-earned savings and highly prized final salary pensions with it.

The 'Stripped of our Pensions' stunt on Brighton beach by workers from the former steel makers Allied Steel & Wire (ASW), followed by one outside Parliament, was part of a concerted high-profile campaign of defiance and resistance. Politicians and civil servants might have preferred to ignore it, but the sight on prime-time television news of middle-aged men posing naked for the cameras was guaranteed to capture the public's imagination. These were forgotten savers, resorting to radical steps to attract the attention of a government which seemed impervious to the desperation of some of its own people. But then perhaps no one should have been surprised. Retirement provision had long been a blind spot of New Labour.

The 1997 raid on pension funds says much about Gordon Brown and his approach to policymaking – secretive, distrustful and dismissive of outside advice. But it also says much about New Labour's general attitude to old age. Government priorities after 1997 were education and the National Health Service. Yet some eight years after it had taken power the same party which increased spending on the NHS from £44 billion when it took office to £100 billion in 2009–10 was neglecting pensions and long-term care for the elderly, even though millions were affected.

For decades occupational schemes such as the one enjoyed by the ASW workers had been an integral part of Britain's pension landscape as a booming stock market boosted returns. Employers shouldered the costs and risks of provision willingly, as actuaries forecast that strong investment returns would fund all the pension commitments. But when Labour MP Frank Field came to look back on a decade of Labour rule he described the scene as 'one of large-scale desolation'.

It would be simplistic to say that everything was healthy until New Labour came along. Years of stock market investment growth had led to overblown valuations of pension funds and the mistaken belief that the long bull market in shares of the 1990s would persist for years to come. In this both employers and employees were complicit, taking too complacent a view of pension surpluses and only too happy to take contribution holidays. But Labour's Budget assault of 1997 could not have been more ill conceived or more poorly timed. It contributed to the severe slump in share prices that came with the 9/11 terrorist attacks and the collapse of the dot.com bubble.

Pension funds were being forced to cope with several challenges. The principle problem was the impact of the Chancellor's raid after 1997. In addition they had to accommodate a whole batch of rules and regulations that added expense and complexity to the running of the schemes. Moreover, these funds were being stretched to provide more generous pensions for widows, greater insurance cover, equal pensions for men and women, and contributions to a compensation scheme for failed funds. As companies facing the economic pinch started to go out of business, the growing problems with their pension funds became painfully exposed.

To make matters worse, flaws were showing in some of the legislation that the Conservatives had brought in towards the end of their period in office. In particular, an unfortunate loophole in the law meant that fund assets could not be ring-fenced. As already mentioned, the original idea was to ensure that schemes had sufficient funds to meet their commitments even if the sponsoring employer went bust. But after strong opposition from some companies, this minimum solvency requirement (MSR), which, apart from anything else would have helped to ring the alarm bells earlier with problematic funds, was watered down and its name changed to minimum funding requirement (MFR).

Under the MFR rule, the wound-up schemes were required to look after existing pensioners first. Staff not yet retired – but with decades of savings invested in the funds – were left to share what was left.

By 2001, the role of the inadequate MFR was being questioned. In a report commissioned by the Treasury, Paul Myners, former chairman of the Gartmore fund management group – who was to be appointed City minister by New Labour in 2008 – called for several measures to tighten pension scheme security. His most controversial recommendation was the abolition of the MFR. He did not believe it protected fund members and argued that removal would encourage schemes to invest in a wider range of companies. The government nevertheless ignored his suggestion.

Two years later, in May 2003, MPs were telling the government that a radical overhaul of the whole regulatory system was needed. The Commons Public Accounts Committee issued a damning report which concluded that both the pension regulator OPRA (set up in 1995 after the Maxwell scandal) and the Department of Work and Pensions were not doing enough to safeguard scheme members. It said that they should be targeting higher-risk schemes.

Pension fund members were still losing out because struggling firms could not be monitored adequately with the MFR. The problem was that while employees were protected against fraud, they still stood to lose most of their pension if their scheme was wound up legally and found to have a shortfall. The fact that they might have been contributing for decades and were close to retirement meant nothing. Malcolm McLean of the Occupational Pensions Advisory Service pointedly noted, 'It matters not to members whether the missing money has been caused by fraud or because a scheme has been voluntarily wound up.'

Technically, of course, private-sector occupational schemes are independent of the state, but ever since the early days of pensions they have been an important component of government planning for old age. Moreover, the state has tended to set the framework in which they operate, even issuing pamphlets to restore trust after the Maxwell and mis-selling scandals. And it was pamphlets such as these that were about to show yet again how cavalier Labour could be.

Despite the deepening problems of private-sector schemes – largely, of course, due to Labour's own actions – the government and its agencies continued in official literature to emphasise pension guarantees and the safety of final salary pensions. Typical in this regard was a guide to pensions issued by the Financial Services Authority in 1999. It failed to mention the dangers attendant upon pension scheme wind-ups. Instead, it referred several times to the benefits of final salary pensions, even going so far as to say that final salary schemes 'give you a guaranteed pension'.

Since New Labour had destroyed the tax regime on which the surpluses of final salary pensions had been built and failed to come clean on the danger of wind-ups for pension scheme members despite being urged to do so, it was, wittingly or unwittingly, misleading the public. Indeed it was engaged in a new version of the pensions mis-selling scandal that had so blighted the Tories' retirement strategy. In the case of the Tories private-sector pension suppliers had been the main culprits. Under Labour it was the government itself which was engaged in a more subtle form of mis-selling. It was providing guarantees and reassurances that, in the event of company collapse, might turn out not to be worth the paper they were written on.

The government consistently ignored advice to issue warnings about the risks involved with pensions. The Treasury had been tipped off; the Department of Social Security was aware of the problem; Pensions Minister Jeff Rooker even admitted in 2000 that the public could get a false impression that the MFR guaranteed solvency. Yet MFR protection was actually weakened in 2002 and OPRA even went so far as to rule that trustees could stop members from leaving schemes, however fragile they knew these schemes to be.

Over the next 12 months the trickle of struggling firms going bust and closing schemes became a flood. More than 80,000 people who had saved into work pension schemes discovered that the MFR and the government's promises of guaranteed retirement provision were all but worthless. As an increasingly long list of companies including ASW, Sea-Land (a division of the conglomerate Maersk), British United Shoe Machinery, Dexion and Samuel Jones went into insolvency, the weaknesses of the regulatory regime and the lack of protection for ordinary employees became ever more obvious. Members were confronted with the realisation that despite saving for many years the pension schemes they belonged to had folded with shortfalls.

ASW was typical of many. Employing 1,300 people and with sites in Cardiff, Sheerness, Kent and Belfast, it had been an independently owned steel company formed in 1981 through a partnership between British Steel and engineering giant GKN. In 1987 the management of the firm bought out the company from the existing owners and it was floated on the stock market a year later.

Unfortunately, the newly floated steel group found itself struggling against adverse market conditions. More than half its output of steel rod and bars was exported to countries in the eurozone, but because of the strength of the pound against the euro its prices were not competitive. Increasing steel production in low-wage economies – in eastern Europe and south Asia – made the situation even worse.

The firm eventually went into receivership on 10 July 2002. A skeleton staff was kept on to wind up the business, while most of the workers at Cardiff – who earned on average over £20,000 a year – lost their jobs. The Cardiff operation later reopened under new Spanish owners Celsa, and when it resumed production around 400 former ASW workers got their jobs back. They did not, however, recover their guaranteed pensions. Today, these once-bustling plants are a pale shadow of what was once a vibrant part of steel making in South Wales.

When ASW folded, word spread quickly that the pension scheme was in deep trouble. Redundant workers hastily arranged a march across Cardiff. Elsewhere others lobbied for support from MPs and government. A hurriedly set up action group went to Downing Street to meet a policy adviser to Tony Blair. It received what was described as no more than 'tea and sympathy'.

The experience of John Benson at ASW was typical. He had joined the firm at 16 and worked his way up to become a team leader at the Cardiff plant. Redundancy came out of the blue and there was no payout. Nevertheless he reassured his wife Linda, 'Don't worry, we'll be fine. I've got a pension.'

He was wrong. In fact, his pension had disappeared into a scheme into which he had contributed for decades:

My father was part of bringing the pension scheme to Allied Steel & Wire some 28 years ago. And he said it was a very good pension. My father told me: 'When the time comes for you to finish work, the money will be there and you won't have a problem. You will have a good retirement.'

Linda, a part-time secretary, could not believe what had happened. 'What do you mean "There's no pension?" There's got to be a pension,' she said to her husband. 'You've paid into that pension scheme and it is your money.' What the Bensons hadn't appreciated was that while government legislation safeguarded existing pensions in the event of a company being wound up, this protection did not extend to those still paying into a scheme. They were condemned to take their chances with what was left.

In recent years Benson, now in his 60s, has been in and out of work, at one stage stacking shelves in a local supermarket, at another baggage handling at Cardiff airport. He accepts he has no hope of ever building up another fund to recreate the £11,000-a-year pension he should have received at 65. 'The future is extremely bleak for me now,' he says. 'If I don't find work, my wife and I will have to sell our home.'

Sue and Gordon MacPherson between them clocked up lengthy service with the firm. Gordon spent 14 years as a storeman, while Sue put in 18 years in the IT department. They were both contributing to the company's pension scheme and, as keen golfers, the couple were hoping to use their pensions to fund their hobby in retirement. Instead, they faced the prospect of being left with next to nothing. They had money saved up, but not enough to live on.

They had opted for the ASW pension scheme on the recommendation of a financial adviser. As far as Sue was concerned there was no warning that things were so bad. As she recalled:

I wasn't worried about the stock market downturn. We had the trustees' report to members and I read all the documents that they sent me. It actually says that nearly half of the assets of the plan are in bonds rather than the stock market. So, I thought, they are obviously looking after the pension fund, there is no need to worry.

Events proved her very wrong.

It was not just traditional industrial businesses like steel that were affected. Dexion, based in the new town of Hemel Hempstead just north of London, which went bust in May 2003, were shelf manufacturers who had had developed a worldwide reputation for their advanced storage and racking systems. Hazel Mackie and her husband James were in their mid-50s when they were made redundant by the firm. As if losing their immediate source of income wasn't bad enough, the couple faced having to survive without the company pension they were expecting. In common with other companies Dexion put its scheme into wind-up with an estimated shortfall of £20 million. A huge shock was in store for the Mackies. Instead of the £20,000 a year they were expecting they had to resign themselves to receiving just £3,000.

Their anger and that of tens of thousands of people like them caught in the same trap was palpable. 'For 36 years, the time that James has belonged to the Dexion pension scheme, we tried to provide for ourselves by contributing to the pension,' said Hazel. 'But now we don't know what to do. Surely James and his colleagues – many of whom have been there as long as him – deserve better. They are ordinary, good family men who have tried to provide for their retirement but who have been let down terribly.'

A government Green Paper in late 2002 stated that accrued pension rights 'are clearly protected in law and this will remain the case'. But when disaster struck ASW in July 2002 and Dexion in April 2003 such promises counted for little. Labour, the party of the working person, looked to have forgotten the principles of care and fairness at the core of its value system. Interestingly, when the banking system imploded a few years later, in 2007–8, the same government responded with alacrity, bailing out the UK banks and guaranteeing savings. It even went so far as to repay savers who had been rash enough to place their money with Icelandic banks for the sake of a few basis points of higher interest. The ASW pensioners and the tens of thousands like them around the country, however, could not hope to look to Westminster or Whitehall for sympathy and support.

Fortunately, though, they did find a powerful ally in the form of Ros Altmann, a fiery and determined independent pension consultant. Altmann – a tall, tanned economic expert from North London – was in many ways an unlikely activist on behalf of dispossessed pensioners. In the early days of New Labour she had been called to service at Downing Street when a root-and-branch reform of pensions was still on the cards. But as the Treasury sought to undermine Tony Blair's initiatives she became increasingly alienated from the government. Her credentials as a pension campaigner were excellent.

A disciple of the future governor of the Bank of England Mervyn King, she had gained her PhD in research on pensions under supervision at the London School of Economics. She had worked at Prudential, managing pension funds and institutional assets in 1982. Later Altmann ran Chase Manhattan Bank's international equity investment division in London. She was a director at Rothschild and NatWest but had stepped down from high-powered life in the City to become an independent financial consultant and to devote more time to family life.

At Number 10 Altmann had been a pensions adviser, working on a review of institutional investment for the Treasury in 2000 and briefing the Number 10 policy unit. She found Downing Street's policy unit sympathetic to her ideas for shaking up Britain's retirement provision but encountered frequent obstruction from the Treasury. Rapidly becoming disillusioned with New Labour's approach to pensions she reverted to her independent consultancy, while later becoming a governor of the London School of Economics and the Pensions Policy Institute.

Altmann believed that the actuarial profession had lost its way. She was convinced that the best way of analysing pension exposure was to use sophisticated new econometric models, and also had carefully worked-out views on how to reduce the investment risks that pension funds faced. Her fierce intellectual approach in some ways made her an unlikely candidate to lead an overtly political campaign against a government to which she had provided advice. But her deep knowledge, and independence, made her a powerful ally to the dispossessed.

At the time of the ASW collapse in 2002 there was no formal compensation scheme for future pensioners caught up in company collapses. The Pension Protection Fund (PPF), designed to bail out pension funds brought to the brink by the collapse of their owners, would not come into force until 2005. It was not open to victims of the early noughties.

The support of the pensions industry for the PPF, lukewarm at best, might have been endangered had the government insisted it accept responsibility for its own past regulatory and managerial mistakes. Consequently, the ASW victims found themselves at the mercy of a scheme which primarily saw its role as dealing with cases of demonstrable hardship, not with those that stemmed from regulatory failure, poorly designed guarantees and the government's own tax follies.

Treasury ministers, headed by Gordon Brown, simply turned a blind eye. They did not share the view that the weakness of company schemes was undermining the robustness of the entire pensions system. Indeed, there was a section of the Treasury that disliked occupational pensions, suspecting that when the public saved for pensions through employers, some clever tax dodge was almost certainly involved. There were even those who, ignoring the vast social range of those in company pensions, assumed that private-sector pensions were some sort of middle-class privilege that could be freely attacked.

A senior Treasury official is quoted by Robert Peston in his 2008 book *Who Runs Britain?* as saying:

> We have a private pension problem. It is a problem for people in the upper-middle bracket. It is to do with expectations and incentives. What we have got all across the country is employers reneging against the implicit contract that the employees thought they had with companies – and the employees not really knowing what to do in the face of that.

Altmann was having none of this. Soon after ASW folded in 2002 she became involved in the campaign to win compensation, saying, 'I thought the steelworkers were such good people – it was so wrong what was happening to them. They put their whole life savings into something which suddenly disappeared and it was clear other people could lose out, too.' She duly spearheaded the formation of the Pensions Action Group (PAG), backing it up with a brilliant publicity initiative and personal lobbying. 'The whole saga,' she declared, 'is an outrage and a monumental betrayal of trust.'

Reflecting on the 'Stripping for Action' campaign, she later said:

> It's the best thing I will ever come up with. We were trying to decide about protests when this big strapping fellow joked that we should all go and take our clothes off in Parliament. I said I hoped they wouldn't and then, realising I might have offended him, thought again and decided why not.

Not for the first time, the government was put in a tricky position. Andrew Smith, the third New Labour minister to hold the title pensions secretary, acknowledged a moral obligation to workers whose retirement aspirations had been shattered. 'When you consider the ASW workers, and other workers who face losing a substantial part of a pension they've been counting on, of course I understand how they feel. It's an awful shock,' he told the BBC's

Panorama programme. But he made it clear that compensating thousands who had lost money when pension schemes collapsed was not an option, arguing for individual responsibility and saying that 'when it comes to investments and markets, there is no such thing as total security'. He did not mention the misleading official literature that so many people had received, or point out that by taking responsibility for their own savings workers were relieving the state of a future burden which would have to be picked up by means testing and other devices.

In the event the government's hard-line stance backfired. It simply prompted protestors to be more vociferous, and eventually Andrew Smith was forced to take some action. Accepting for the first time that perhaps the state did have some kind of financial responsibility to those whose pensions had collapsed, in May 2004 the government offered limited compensation in the form of the Financial Assistance Scheme (FAS), run by the Department for Work and Pensions.

The groups entitled to compensation under the scheme were narrowly defined and the money derisory. Victims had to be members of an underfunded defined benefit scheme that started to wind up between 1 January 1997 and 5 April 2005. If they were within seven years of their scheme retirement age they would, at 65, receive around 80 per cent of their accrued rights at the point at which either they left the scheme or it began to wind up. If they were seven to ten years away they would receive 65 per cent, and if they were twelve years or more away a mere 50 per cent. There would be no indexation or payments to dependents.

The Smith concessions may have won ministers a little time, but the Pensions Action Group was unimpressed, arguing that the compensation proposals left many of its members out in the cold. It was also suggested that the FAS, designed to assist in a few hardship cases, was inadequately staffed and resourced and far too bureaucratic. Persuading it to release funds threatened to be a humiliating experience and as excruciating as pulling teeth.

Ros Altmann proposed an alternative that would give the victims a better deal. Instead of using a collapsed fund to buy annuities she proposed that assets should be left in the scheme and paid out as pensions as they became due each week. Of course the funds would run out eventually, but Altmann estimated that it would be 'a large number of years' before they did so. She argued, 'If these people are forced to court, they will win anyway, but it will end up then costing the taxpayer a lot more money.'

Altmann's continuing campaign was accompanied by the threat of legal action by workers and their unions. They argued the government was ignoring part of the 1980 European Union Insolvency Directive that 'requires member states to ensure that there are necessary measures in place to protect employees in relation to their pension rights'. The ISTC union threatened to sue the government over the collapse of ASW, which had left its members with only 10 per cent of the previous value of their pension fund. An additional challenge was being prepared, also on human rights grounds, by the Welsh Nationalist Party Plaid Cymru, many of whose constituents worked at the Cardiff plants.

The legal, media and political pressure was getting to the government, and in April 2005 it came up with fresh proposals. This time it announced that the newly formed Pension Protection Fund (PPF) would act as a safety net covering final salary schemes. The PPF would provide £2.9 billion of assistance to compensate members of collapsed schemes under terms similar to those of the FAS. It was good news for victims of recent cases of insolvency, but it quickly became clear that the legislation would not be retrospective and that the victims of ASW and the other pre-2005 wind-up schemes would not be covered.

Further pressure was coming the Government's way. In March 2006 the parliamentary ombudsman Ann Abraham published the report of her 18-month inquiry into claims that the government misled workers over the security of their pensions, focusing on the cases of some 85,000 people who had lost part or all of their pensions when their employers abandoned their occupational schemes. Her conclusion was damning. Describing government information on occupational pensions as 'inaccurate', 'incomplete', 'unclear' and 'inconsistent', she laid an accusation of mal-administration at their door. This was a telling word to use. In 1989 a similar ruling by one of her predecessors in the case of investment firm Barlow Clowes had led to full government compensation for all the savers that had been damaged.

The ombudsman, whose reports on Equitable Life would emerge in subsequent years, was one of the few public servants brave enough to hold New Labour to account over its neglectful approach to those who had lost their supposedly properly regulated retire-ment savings through no fault of their own. Abraham's report quoted the prime minister's foreword to the ministerial code, which referred to the 'bond of trust' between the British people and their government. 'It seems to me that citizens should be entitled to expect that the publications of official bodies . . . do not mislead them,' she added. Abraham concluded that official leaflets did not make it clear that the schemes were still not totally safe and did not give employees the opportunity to spread their risks.

My colleague Tony Hazell, writing in the *Daily Mail*, summed up the public mood at the time:

It cannot be emphasised too strongly that these people are not layabouts or scroungers. It was not their desire to be going cap in hand to the Government. They worked hard and saved hard, putting an average of £50,000 into their pensions.

He added:

This report is a damning indictment of successive governments who, again and again, gave misleading information about the safety of pensions and failed to protect the interests of long-term investors. Now, as tens of thousands endure lives blighted by the failure of their pensions, the Government is once again refusing to accept responsibility.

Hazell could also have noted that many of those concerned were working-class core Labour voters betrayed by a government which seemed to have convinced itself that occupational pensions – far from being a prudent form of saving for millions of Britons – were a luxury the nation could not afford.

In a public response to the ombudsman's findings, the seventh New Labour secretary of state for pensions John Hutton repeated the familiar mantra that the government was not responsible for pension fund losses and that the taxpayer should not be asked to pick up the bill. Fund performance, he argued, was the responsibility of the trustees. He added, 'Our leaflets never said that the pensions promises of employers were guaranteed – neither by the Government nor the taxpayer . . . it has never been the state's role to underwrite private saving.'

Nevertheless, in May 2006 the government conceded more ground. It revealed that it would boost the financial help given to employees who had lost their pensions when schemes went bust or ceased to exist. A pensions White Paper contained details of improvements to the FAS, which would have its funding increased from £400 million to £2.3 billion. The scheme would be extended so that a further 22,000 people – in addition to a previously identified 30,000 – could benefit from the bail-out.

Two years after Andrew Smith had first boosted the FAS there were still many examples of real hardship. A report in October 2006 highlighted the plight of Michael Eaglestone, by then 65, who had worked as a welder with Dexion for 34 years. Shortly before his 60th birthday – when he planned to retire – the company asked him to stay on because it needed his skills. Before agreeing to do so, he checked the government literature and satisfied himself that his £10,000-a-year pension was safe. His wife Audrey confirmed: 'If my husband had any inkling of the coming situation or the possibility of losing his pension, there is no way he would have carried on.'

Dexion went bust a few weeks before his 62nd birthday. By not retiring at 60, Eaglestone's pension was lost. Struggling with ill health, he eked out a living by stacking shelves at night in a supermarket, before discovering from the Dexion fund trustees that there was only enough money in the pot to pay him a pension of £50 a week. His situation was made worse by the fact that he had contracted out so had lost his state-related entitlement in the Dexion scheme. Despite applying three times to the FAS, Eaglestone had not received a penny in compensation.

Ros Altmann was outraged:

The government misled him and prevented him from taking the decision that would have secured his pension. If he had been told the truth about the effect of the legal priority order introduced by the government, and also about the weakness of the official standards for pensions, he would not have delayed retirement.

Within weeks, startling figures showed that Eaglestone's story was echoed throughout the country. Despite the extra funding for the FAS and the setting up of the more robust Pension Protection Fund in April 2007, some 125,000 people who had lost their pensions when their final salary schemes failed were still fighting for justice. The government faced widespread calls for emergency funding so that loans could be issued to trustees to pay PPF-level pensions. Pressure groups such as the Occupational Pensioners' Alliance argued that money in failed funds could be pooled to establish a 'Pension Restoration Fund' and be topped up with orphan assets from insurance companies.

It was not until the end of 2007, years after the scandal had emerged and after untold hardship and emotional stress for the workers involved, that the government finally gave in to the pressure and announced further concessions. The eighth senior minister to fill the role of pensions secretary, Peter Hain, told the Commons on 17 December that up to 140,000 workers who had lost their money in schemes would now see 90 per cent of their pensions restored by the government. The move followed intense behind-the-scenes lobbying by Altmann, who found Hain – a politician who had come to prominence decades earlier as an anti-apartheid campaigner – more sympathetic and understanding of the issues than most of his predecessors.

Hain was also willing to do battle with the Treasury over the request for increased funding. As a result of his intervention, some 800 steelworkers at ASW who had lost their jobs when the firm went out of business were brought into the rescue scheme and offered the same compensation as those covered by the newly created PPF, which was largely funded by a levy on healthy private-sector funds. Hain said that the money, mainly to come from taxpayers, would deliver justice to workers 'cruelly robbed' of their pensions.

Former ASW worker Brian Silver was relieved at the announcement. He had been expecting an annual pension of £12,000, which dropped to an estimated £1,500 when he was made redundant. 'It has been a long, hard road over the past five or so years,' he said. 'We started off our campaign saying that we should receive 100 per cent, but sometimes you fall short of what you expect. You plan for your retirement and it was put on hold, but now we can get back on track.'

It had been a long haul and one that reflected appallingly on the Labour government, which had to be dragged kicking and screaming to the rescue. But it was not the only such scandal to occur on their watch.

CHAPTER 7

The Equitable iniquity

Les and Shirley Crouch were enjoying life to the full. Comfortably off in retirement, they had many friends, a nice house and plenty of carefree leisure time. Holidays abroad were enlivened by visits to such top international sporting events as the Commonwealth Games and the World Athletics Championships. On the cards was a trip to the Beijing Olympics spectacular in 2008.

There was a problem on the horizon, however. Les, a former transport executive, had invested in a pension pot with Britain's oldest provider, Equitable Life.

In the course of 1999 unsettling media stories began to circulate about Equitable Life's financial health. Then, the following year, things moved on to an altogether new and critical level. Forced to close its doors to new business, the society found itself on the brink of failure, with insufficient assets to meet its commitments.

Les, who was 70 at the time, saw his pension halved almost overnight. This would eventually force him and Shirley, who was 65, to economise by moving from their five-bedroom Cardiff house to a smaller home in a cheaper area, switching to a much smaller car, and cutting out theatre visits and overseas holidays. The trip to Beijing was soon a forgotten dream. By the spring of 2009, his pension payout had fallen from £800 a month to £300 a month.

Moreover, the couple felt isolated. As Les commented ruefully:

We had to say goodbye to any hopes of a comfortable

retirement. We have even had to stop going to the theatre with friends, which we love doing. And as we socialised less to save money, our circle of friends dwindled. We had become the poor relations. Maybe people felt sorry for us, but we found we were being left out of the loop when friends were planning anything.

He had little doubt who bore the responsibility for many of his woes: 'The government ripped me off and they have been playing hardball for the last eight years, refusing to accept the blame.'

In fairness, the government was not to blame for the mess that Equitable got itself into. What is certainly the case, though, is that once Equitable's problems became known, New Labour's muddled, ineffectual and at times deliberately obstructive response made a very bad situation far, far worse.

The great tragedy was that Equitable had such an impressive pedigree. It had started life in 1762 as the Society for Equitable Assurances on Lives and Survivorships – or the Equitable Life Assurance Society – and throughout its history it had developed innovative products. Indeed, the insurer's very origins resulted from pioneering work by a fellow of the Royal Society, James Dodson, who some 12 years earlier had revolutionised the way that life assurance worked through developing a scientific basis for calculating premiums.

Dodson used mortality rates and probability studies to calculate tables of fair annual premiums. The great advantages of these tables were that the policyholder's premium was fixed throughout the term of the policy and the amount paid on death was guaranteed. Dodson actually died before Equitable was founded, but his ideas formed the basis upon which all modern life assurance schemes were subsequently built.

Within 15 years of its formation, Equitable was able to cut all premiums by 10 per cent. Another reduction in premiums followed in 1781 and a regular system of bonuses was subsequently developed.

The combination of fair dealing and reasonable bonuses rapidly attracted new business, and by 1799 there were 5,000 policies in force for sums totalling around £4 million. By 1810 membership was approaching 10,000. Notable policyholders of the time included such leading figures as the poet Samuel Taylor Coleridge, social reformer William Wilberforce and writer Sir Walter Scott.

The end of the nineteenth century saw another period of rapid growth for Equitable, and in 1913 the society began selling pensions. Again the society was able to boast some notable members, including writer John Galsworthy, politician Neville Chamberlain and cricketer W. G. Grace. In 1957 it built on its reputation for innovation by launching the 'Retirement Annuity' – a flexible pension for the self-employed. Corporate pension scheme members came to include such familiar names as the National Health Service, multinational giant Unilever and the Post Office.

Equitable's ultimate downfall stemmed from controversial business strategies devised in the 1980s and 1990s. Success started to beget overconfidence and a willingness to indulge in risk-taking. In feeding the voracious appetite for personal finance products, Equitable sought to exploit the white-hot market atmosphere of the time. Consumers were lured in by the company's leading personal pension plan and its management of additional voluntary contributions (AVCs). These are a form of top-up pension offered by companies to employees who wanted to save extra for retirement, with employers often offering matching contributions. The attractions of Equitable Life as a manager were that it had a record as a good manager of assets, it did not pay fat commissions to its sales force and it offered unrivalled guarantees.

On the surface, Equitable appeared able to provide a better return on its funds than its competitors. The insurer claimed that part of the reason why it was in a position to achieve this was that its operating costs were very low: by selling policies through its own sales force, it was able to cut out commission fees to financial advisers. (That said, its own salespeople gained a reputation for being among the highest earners in the financial services industry.)

At its height Equitable was one of the biggest mutually owned life insurers in the world, with around 1.5 million policyholders. But its success rested on two extremely dodgy financial foundations: large bonuses for policyholders and guaranteed annuity sums.

The roots of the 'over-bonusing' catastrophe can be traced to 1989, when Equitable had again been first in the market by publishing a business plan called 'With Profits, Without Mystery' as the model for its pensions strategy. The publication's title would later prove ironic but it was a great sales device at the time. It appealed to potential investors by presenting its case in glossy brochure form, dispensing with the usual insurance jargon and presenting the policy fundamentals in a simple way. Gone was the dry-as-dust impenetrable world of insurance. To the average investor, the business plan represented a touch of glamour wedded to a businesslike approach, which created a feel-good factor.

What Equitable was offering was not only attractively packaged – it read well and looked good – but appeared to deliver the goods too. Traditionally, insurers have prudently set bonuses at less than their profits, thus building up reserves. These often-huge surpluses are sometimes described as orphan assets. Such funds are accumulated over decades, long after particular policies have matured. They enable insurers to match bonuses with profits over an extended period of time. Assets and liabilities may of course vary over this period, but the accumulated surpluses allow everything to be 'smoothed'. In the long term, everything should then balance.

In an unprecedented move, Equitable decided to turn this formula on its head and distribute bonuses that matched its current assets. Its business plan proudly announced that as profits were made, linked with day-to-day stock market performance, so bonuses would be declared. Smoothing effectively went out of the window. The appointed actuary at Equitable in the 1990s, the horn-rim-spectacled Chris Headdon, later described this approach to the inquiry judge as 'smoothing across the peaks'. Judge Penrose, who headed the probe, was less impressed.

When Equitable first came up with this bold plan, its proposals took the actuarial industry by surprise. One industry professional said it would only work as long as the books were carefully and constantly balanced. This is precisely what Equitable would fail to do.

The scheme had hardly begun when the stock market went into reverse. The bonuses, however, still kept coming. With assets falling and policy values rising, a huge gap started to open up. New business was pouring in but without the assets in place to support it. Moreover, a significant part of the new business was immediately diverted to members whose policies were maturing. If a new policyholder set up a £10,000 pension pot, for example, £1,000 would actually go to paying out someone else.

Equitable was effectively voting bonuses out of assets it didn't have. In 2001 pensions expert Professor David Blake of City University's Cass Business School described the society's business model as 'having similarities with the Ponzi scheme' of the early 1900s.

Ponzi schemes, which involved an elaborate form of pyramid selling, would become familiar again in 2008–9, when the nefarious activities of former Nasdaq chairman and titan of Wall Street investment Bernard Madoff were revealed in the United States. Madoff was able to produce strangely regular returns of 8 to 9 per cent for investors through even the most turbulent market conditions and the ups and downs of the trade cycle.

Faced with a severe problem, Equitable used accounting ingenuity to improve the look of its books: it decided to 'weaken the valuation' by reducing the book value of its liabilities. It did so by what accountant Colin Slater, himself an Equitable policyholder, called 'a clever piece of discounted cash-flow work, which the regulators put through on the nod'.

It worked as follows. According to annual statements, Policyholder X had a fund worth £100,000 plus a terminal bonus –

paid when the policy matures at the end of its time span – possibly worth another £20,000. However, when Equitable valued this policy for the regulators, it argued that as Policyholder X was 40 – and so 20 years off retirement – his £100,000 would not have to be met for another 20 years. Consequently, Equitable was able to indulge in some clever maths that involved discounting at 10 per cent and adding a bonus at 3 per cent, the end result being the magical valuation figure of £50,000. 'If policyholders had seen such a discrepancy in the figures they would have had hysterics,' says Slater.

In 1990 Equitable had assets of £5 billion, a relatively small balance sheet in insurance company terms. But with regulators accepting the 'down-valuation', the society was able to go on declaring bonuses out of profits it didn't have. This in turn attracted hundreds of thousands of new customers. By the time it all went wrong – at the end of the decade – the society's assets had ballooned six-fold to £30 billion.

Over-bonusing was a big problem for Equitable. But there was an even larger one looming in the shape of guaranteed annuity rates (or GAR). These promised a particular rate of annuity – 7 per cent – on retirement, and also allowed investors to retire at any of the dates that were open to them in line with the tax rules – a window of opportunity stretching over 15 years.

When Equitable set its annuity levels at 7 per cent in the 1970s this seemed safe enough: inflation was raging and interest rates were correspondingly high. But from 1982 they fell steeply, and by the mid-1990s interest rates to support annuity rates were actually down to the level that Equitable was guaranteeing. Britain's exit from the Exchange Rate Mechanism in September 1992 and the establishment of 'inflation targeting' by the Bank of England combined to produce a seismic change in interest rate and inflation patterns. Equitable found itself stuck with pension promises that it could no longer fulfil, made worse by the fact that it had also made no provision for the crisis. 'This was a problem – a fundamental miscalculation – that just grew,' explains Colin Slater. 'Having set the annuity rates at below market rates in the 70s, Equitable never expected it [the guarantee] to come into play.'

To make matters worse Equitable had introduced a terminal bonus along the way. It looked very attractive: would-be investors were offered the prospect of a guaranteed annuity rate plus a bonus on retirement, with the whole pension pot paid out at the guaranteed rate. What was not fully spelled out was that Equitable intended paying the guaranteed rate only on the annuity. The terminal bonus was never covered by the guarantee and no provision had been made for it. Furthermore, Equitable planned to deduct the costs of providing guarantees from the terminal bonus amount. In other words investors could have a guaranteed rate on either their annuity or the terminal bonus, but not both.

The society's actuaries had worked out as far back as 1983 what they intended doing if GAR became a problem, but they didn't tell the regulators of their intentions until 1993, and policyholders somewhat later. 'There was no clue for investors along the way,' says Slater. 'Even accountants would have had difficulty understanding the published figures, so what chance policyholders? They had to assume that regulators had OK'd the figures on their behalf.'

With growing problems rumbling beneath the surface, Equitable was still focused on developing new business and going for growth. Much of the responsibility for the expansion policy can be placed at the door of the domineering figure of Roy Ranson, who as key executive brooked no dissent. He was the society's actuary between 1982 and 1997, when many of the controversial products were designed, taking over as managing director in 1991, a post he held until his retirement in 1997. As the architect of the collapse, he was eventually expelled from the Institute of Actuaries in 2007. His successor, Alan Nash, a stout, overconfident man with a shock of black hair, was still selling the Equitable recovery story long after 1999–2000, when the writing was on the wall.

The first signs that Equitable was in trouble over guaranteed annuity rates came in 1999, when the society's management took a test case to the High Court, seeking to validate its attempt to turn its back on its GAR policy and wriggle out of the promise it had made to certain policyholders over many years. After the first hearing in July judges backed the society's right to cut bonuses. But policyholders took the issue to appeal. In January 2000, the Appeal Court reversed the decision, ruling that Equitable must honour its original commitments.

Equitable's response was to take the matter to the highest court in the land, the House of Lords. In July 2000 the Lords ruled that the society could not abandon its commitment. Moreover, it emerged that the insurer would need to put aside an extra £1.5 billion to make good its promise on GAR.

Equitable did not have this sort of money so it put itself up for sale, initially demanding £5 billion but eventually offering to accept just one pound if several billions were then made available by the purchaser. There were no takers. When potential buyers, like the Prudential, looked at the figures, they could see all too clearly that there was a colossal black hole in the books. Even though Equitable had one of the most desirable rolls of policyholders in the nation – including many of the great and the good – a rescue takeover was considered too expensive.

With no buyer forthcoming and on the verge of collapse, the society closed its doors to new business on 8 December 2000. The society's president, John Sclater – who stepped down in 2001 – was appalled at the turn of events. In a personal statement he offered 'a most sincere apology' to policyholders and employees, though over-optimistically also leaving the impression that a sale of some of the insurer's operations would mean that some value could be recaptured for victims of the collapse and that operations would continue offering 'the best service to policyholders'.

The only way Equitable could now survive was by paying investors in line with what the underlying funds were really worth. Those still paying into policies found their value slashed by the new management. Those who had already retired but had kept their funds invested in with-profits policies – the so-called 'with profits annuitants' – suffered even more. Their money was trapped in the society and their pension payments too were slashed, partly because underlying funds were moved into safer but much-lower-yielding bond funds.

By 2000 the stated value of Equitable customers' policies was £3 billion more than the assets actually held by the company. A new board was drafted in, headed by Florence-born Vanni Treves, a well-connected City lawyer and senior partner at Macfarlanes LLP. He was among the injured parties who had saved for a pension with Equitable Life. Treves, an urbane figure who was well known in media circles as the chairman of broadcaster Channel 4, took on the chairman's role at Equitable on 2 February out of a sense of duty to his fellow policyholders.

He brought with him other high-profile 'fixers' such as Charles Thomson, a refugee from Scottish Widows, who became chief executive, and Charles Bellringer, who became finance director.

Treves was determined to resolve Equitable's troubles and stuck commendably to the task. He was, however, given a rough ride. Thousands of policyholders who lost money when the insurer crashed sent him hate mail and, as the new face of the failed insurer, he even found excrement in his letterbox. It was only later that he received his due as the man who turned the insurer's fortunes around and fought for the interests of members affected by the collapse.

At the beginning of the rescue process Treves had to be the constant bearer of bad news. A year after the society closed its doors, he revealed that the cash shortfall was actually £4.4 billion. This startling disclosure forced the new board to slash policy values and to make plans to sell off the Equitable's operations to generate cash to pay policyholders. The Halifax bank eventually paid £1 billion to purchase Equitable's sales force and non-profit policies, bringing in a £250 million injection of funds in February 2002.

Next, greater exit penalties were introduced for withdrawing funds. In response investors formed action groups, and a rash of compromise deals were discussed in an attempt to stave off legal action. Even so, in July 2001 with-profits policyholders learned that their savings would be slashed by 16 per cent. By the autumn Equitable was seeking a deal which offered to increase the value of plans, but this required GAR policyholders to sign away guaranteed pension rights and non-GAR investors to drop legal claims.

In May 2006 Equitable was able to announce a deal to transfer £4.6 billion of non-profit pension annuities to rival insurer Canada Life. Six months later it sold its wholly owned subsidiary University Life to Reliance Mutual for an undisclosed sum. Just over a year later Equitable agreed to transfer £1.8 billion of with-profits annuity policies to the Prudential. With large parts of the business sold, Equitable had become considerably smaller than it had been at its peak. Even so, it still had 200,000 individual policyholders and 300,000 members of group pension schemes invested in its £6.5 billion with-profits fund. Ever a realist, Treves wanted to sell the rump of the Equitable business and, despite the tough markets, various bidders lined up for the society's remaining £7 billion of assets.

In August 2008 Treves confirmed there were three front runners – 'all major big insurers' (reported to be Swiss Re, Prudential and Legal & General) – wanting to run the pension schemes of Equitable's 500,000 policyholders. 'We won't sell if independence offers a better, safer route for Equitable,' Treves said. 'The measure must be what's in the interests of policyholders. The market for closed insurance books is incredibly good at the moment. There is Hugh Osmond's Pearl and Mark Wood's Paternoster and several other outfits looking to buy.'

Within four months all had changed. The global financial crisis of the autumn destroyed the valuation of financial assets, and the sale of the remains of Equitable was called off in late 2008. Treves, however, thought the overall strategy of slimming down the operation had been correct. He believed it had been a hugely fulfilling and worthwhile project that helped rescue thousands of pensions.

No one can be in any doubt as to the architects of Equitable's downfall. From the 1980s onwards, Equitable's management adopted an aggressive and highly risky strategy that involved making promises that they were not able to keep. Their long-term planning for what was, after all, a long-term business was lamentable.

But while the blame for Equitable's initial difficulties lies fairly and squarely with its management, a fair measure of blame for the way that things then spiralled out of control has to be laid at the door of New Labour.

No government has ever been able totally to ignore private pension provision – if nothing else, it has major implications for the way that state pensions are organised. Not surprisingly, therefore, successive governments have taken on ever greater regulatory powers, particularly after the Maxwell and mis-selling scandals of the 1990s.

Up until 1997, under the Conservatives, supervision of pension providers was split between various departments. The old Department of Trade and Industry (DTI) – or the 'Department of Timidity and Ineptitude' as it was wryly known – took responsibility, along with the Treasury, for the regulation of insurance companies that sold long-term investment products. The section within the DTI with immediate responsibility for ensuring firms were solvent was known as the Insurance Directorate. Expertise in the intricacies of insurance largely resided in the Government Actuaries Department (GAD), which provided technical support in the regulation of life insurers, offering analysis on risk and scrutinising the regulatory returns of providers like Equitable.

In his report on the collapse of Equitable published in 2004 Lord Penrose concluded, 'It is clear that Equitable's returns were not understood by the GAD actuaries throughout the 1990s.' According to Colin Slater, the DTI and GAD had a split system in which one arm knew all the numbers and the other arm was there to regulate, which was exactly why regulation didn't work. 'GAD and the DTI didn't talk to each other. And even if they did, they wouldn't have understood each other.'

GAD's initial mistake was to allow Ranson to retain his post as the appointed actuary when he took over as chief executive. These roles are normally kept separate to avoid any conflict of interest. Ranson was both the internal regulator of the company and protector of policyholders' interests and the promoter of the society's ambitious expansion policy. Ranson continued in this joint role despite what Penrose called 'the obvious dangers inherent in such a concentration of authority and influence'.

Even so, signs of potential insolvency at Equitable were there for GAD and the DTI to see in 1990, when Equitable reduced the value of all its liabilities by hundreds of millions of pounds after running short of money through voting bonuses for savers seemingly out of thin air. Surprisingly, the government actuaries agreed to the move, presumably believing Equitable was solvent. For many businesses solvency is a matter of being able to pay the wages or the creditors at the end of the month. Insurance companies, on the other hand, have large sums of money invested and longer time horizons. For them, solvency is being able to pay the policy values when they mature in 10 or 20 years' time. GAD must have thought Equitable could.

In May 1997 responsibility for Equitable passed to New Labour and to a new supervisory set-up. In one of the government's first moves Chancellor Gordon Brown reformed financial regulation in Britain by setting up a tripartite system involving the Bank of England, the Treasury and the newly formed Financial Services Authority. As part of Brown's preparations to establish the FSA as a single financial services regulator, the Treasury became involved in insurance regulation and took on staff from the DTI's Insurance Directorate. From January 1998 the Treasury was directly responsible for the prudential regulation of insurance companies, and then a year later contracted out the day-to-day supervision to the FSA, which had the task of keeping a watchful eye on Equitable.

The tripartite system was to show itself woefully inadequate – not least in its inability to predict and forestall the 2007 collapse of Northern Rock and the ensuing bank crisis – nevertheless, the Treasury did at least soon recognise Equitable as a problem case. Within months of Labour's accession to power a meeting was arranged at which the society was told to get its balance sheet in order. The Treasury wanted to see a bigger provision, running into billions of pounds, to meet the problem of the Equitable's guaranteed annuity rate, and it was instructed not to pay a bonus.

The society pointed out that if policyholders discovered that they were not to receive a bonus for 1998 there would be real trouble. Consequently a compromise was reached by which the society was allowed to take out a reinsurance contract to secure its future liabilities.

Normally such an arrangement – much like a bookmaker laying off a bet in horse racing – means the reinsurer takes on the risk.

Unfortunately, in this case most reinsurers felt the risk was too rich for them: policyholders were likely to take their guaranteed annuities within years and the interest rate that underpinned the basic promise to investors had been breached. In insurance terms, the risk was already out in the open – the option being, in industry jargon, 'in the money'. The proposition from Equitable facing reinsurers has been likened to a property developer asking for cover for a block of flats when a fire has already engulfed the first and second floors.

Eventually, though, an offshore insurance company, the Irish Reinsurance Corporation (part of America's General Electric), was found, which agreed to a £700,000 premium. This contract allowed Equitable to claim it now had an asset worth £700 million to help cover the gap in its liabilities. Equitable went ahead and declared its bonus for the year, and its figures for the year were approved by the regulators.

Coming up with reinsurance, though, was no more than tinkering at the margins of the problem. Indeed, policyholders have since described the scheme as 'not worth the paper it was written on'. New Labour's shiny new policeman was proving as ineffectual in its supervision as its predecessors at the DTI and the Treasury. 'When the FSA took over responsibility, the same people from GAD and the DTI were involved – all that changed was the nameplate on the door outside,' says Colin Slater. 'The FSA has only ever been concerned to cover its backside.' Indeed, there is reason to believe that the people placed in charge at the FSA lacked the necessary experience in supervising insurance companies.

More seriously, the FSA's actions in 1997 arguably made it complicit in Equitable's problems, desire to keep things secret and claim to have £700 million in extra assets to cover any shortfalls. Indeed, the FSA directors actually overruled their actuaries when the latter questioned the advisability of the reinsurance policy. Equitable continued selling business to the tune of £2 billion to £3 billion a year – the high point of their sales – apparently attracting more and more people on the basis of ever-flimsier numbers. Even when the society was put up for sale and closed to new business, the FSA maintained – in public at least – that the company was solvent and that it complied with all regulatory requirements.

One object of the FSA leadership under Sir Howard Davies – the former deputy governor of the Bank of England parachuted in by the government – was to douse any panic. One policyholder commented, 'The FSA let them get away with it. This was pure nonsense. The regulators connived in what went on at Equitable. They actively conspired to keep the society going and ensure it could happen.'

Regulators assumed no one would be disadvantaged when Equitable continued selling policies after 1999. They appeared to assume there would be compensation if something went wrong.

There was no recognition that new victims were being sucked into the morass or that other policyholders would have to pay the compensation. There was no attempt to quantify the risks of Equitable continuing to do business, and no attempt to mitigate the possibility that policyholders might in future claim misrepresentation. The Penrose Report would later find that there was an 'unacceptable' overall lack of coordination between the two branches of regulation – the DTI, responsible for 'prudential regulation' of the company's solvency, and other regulators checking on whether it followed strict rules on the selling process. In the words of Lord Penrose, there was a 'general failure on the part of regulators and GAD to mount effective challenge of the management'.

The FSA carefully monitored the unfolding nightmare in the courts as policyholders sued Equitable. The politically savvy first chairman, Howard Davies, and the former Bank of England official now in charge of the supervision of complex financial institutions, Michael Foot, recognised they could soon be facing the first test of the Brown regulatory structure. Foot was confident the crisis could be quietly handled. An ebullient and optimistic official, he told me over lunch at the time that it could simply be a matter of closing the insurer to new business and placing it into run-off . Companies in run-off no longer take on new business and seek to settle obligations to policyholders as they fall due from ring-fenced assets.

There was a long history of insurance failures being handled in this way. This sounded sensible enough. But Equitable Life was no ordinary insurer. It had over-promised to policyholders and failed to accumulate the cushion of reserves and unallocated assets which were a feature of most insurance accounts. It was effectively bust.

After the collapse there was a flurry of parliamentary hearings and court cases as attempts were made to deal with the dire situation faced by the company and its policyholders. On the surface there appeared to be a real sense of urgency about resolving the matter. In truth the Blair government was more worried about the inevitable finger-pointing that would follow any proper investigation. It wasn't really concerned with helping the victims.

What followed therefore was an exercise in prevarication. The government paid lip service to the public clamour to sort things out but, prompted by Brown and the Treasury, adopted a go-slow approach. It is well known that if a government wants to avoid taking action, it commissions a report, and that's precisely what New Labour did for the next eight years. Fearful of the cost to the exchequer of any compensation awarded to Equitable victims and the precedent it might set, Gordon Brown, first as chancellor and then as prime minister, helped ensure that the issue was consistently kicked into the long grass.

In point of fact, the first inquiry – by Ronnie Baird, the FSA's internal auditor – was remarkably swift and to the point, seeing the light of day in October 2001. Baird looked into how the newly minted FSA had handled the affair from January 1999 to December 2000, along with the Personal Investment Authority ombudsman (later folded into the FSA) and the Treasury. He concluded that the FSA failed to spot key problems and to follow up issues that had been uncovered. In particular, he was critical of the FSA's decision to allow Equitable to disguise its problems by arranging an expensive reinsurance contract negotiated by its former managing director Chris Heddon. And he reprimanded the FSA for the decision to allow the Equitable to recruit new members – future victims – when the scale of its problems was already evident. Nevertheless, Baird felt the 'die was cast' before the FSA took over regulation.

The government hoped that this would be the end of the matter. But they reckoned without the ceaseless campaigning of the Equitable Members Action Group (EMAG), other lobby groups, prominent Equitable Life policyholders and intense interest in the financial press. Consequently it was announced in October 2001 that an eminent judge, Lord Penrose, would conduct an inquiry into the collapse of the society. This time things proceeded in a satisfactorily slow and stately manner. Penrose was careful and deliberate in his work, and at times seemed to be struggling with the extraordinarily complex actuarial issues at the heart of the Equitable debacle. His calls for ever more files and papers, going back over generations of policies, raised questions as to whether his investigation would ever be completed and whether he was capable of actually producing a meaningful report. He was said to have become mired in the theology of actuarial calculations.

As the probe dragged on, the frustration of policyholders – some of whom would tragically die in the interim – was palpable. When the Penrose report did finally appear in March 2004, it was a damp squib. The judge failed to come up with the clear-cut answers that policyholders had been hoping for. The volume of evidence and the technical detail at the heart of the inquiry seemed to have got the better of him.

Lord Penrose's report did point to regulatory failings. However, it argued that the blame for Equitable's problems lay principally with the society's management. Penrose confirmed that for many years they had been telling its savers that their accumulated funds were worth far more than was really the case. The society had simply failed to put enough money away in its reserves for a rainy day, allocating far too much of the return on its investment funds to paying members immediately. Penrose estimated that the society had told its investors their policies were worth £3 billion more than was actually the case. On top of this there was a £1.5 billion bill for the GAR fiasco. The report said that the society had used 'dubious' actuarial techniques to make it appear profitable when it was actually losing money. It also identified what it saw as a 'culture of concealment and manipulation' within the company. Penrose concluded: 'Equitable used a range of dubious actuarial techniques to make it look like it made a surplus, when it had, in fact, made a loss.'

Gordon Brown, then chancellor and the Cabinet minister who was directly responsible, excused himself from commenting on the report on the grounds that a somewhat distant family member happened to be an Equitable Life policyholder. It was left to Ruth Kelly, a junior Treasury minister with a good understanding of economics but precious little experience in financial regulation, to present selected findings of the report to the Commons in March 2004. In a stony-faced, monotone presentation Kelly emphasised the company's own role in its misfortunes and minimised regulatory neglect.

This did not end the clamour for justice, and pressure grew for further action to establish a case of maladministration. In the Barlow Clowes case more than a decade earlier a finding of maladministration by the ombudsman had proved the trigger for the Tory government to compensate investors let down by faulty supervision.

Parliamentary Ombudsman Ann Abraham had already issued a report in July 2003 – before the release of Penrose – in which she cleared the FSA of any wrongdoing. But in her second – weighty – report in 2008 she decided to focus on the charge of mal-administration and not stray into the numbers. Her 2,819-page document duly found that the regulators had failed to protect policyholders. They had let the society continue trading 'on an unsound basis' for a decade, thus letting the public be misled into thinking the society was solvent when it was not. Abrahams gave ten examples of maladministration by the authorities and called for the government to establish a compensation scheme:

> The Government should establish and fund a compensation scheme to assess the losses of individuals, and they should set up a scheme that's independent, which is transparent and which is simple. That should happen speedily – within two years of a decision to set up a scheme

Up until now the government had consistently resisted calls for compensation, fearing that the bill might run into billions of pounds. But the pressure on ministers following the second Abraham Report was too great to resist. In January 2009 Treasury Chief Secretary Yvette Cooper made a grudging apology in the Commons over the Equitable collapse. Ex-gratia payments, she said, would be made, but only to people who were 'disproportionately affected'. This group was never fully defined but it came to be regarded 'as those who suffered most'.

In the heated debate that followed, Cooper offered an apology to MPs for the failures of regulators and successive governments between 1990 and 2000. She refused to say when compensation would be paid, how much would be involved or who would get it. Repeated attempts by MPs to get her to set a timetable were brushed aside. The minister simply said payments would be made 'as swiftly as possible'.

Paradoxically, Cooper would be shuffled out of the Treasury shortly afterwards, in May 2009, and given a seat in the Cabinet as secretary of state for work and pensions. Despite its core responsibilities for the unemployed and the elderly this had proved to be one of the least valued jobs under New Labour, with the door spinning so quickly that often it has proved near impossible to remember who the minister is at any given moment, let alone what their pensions policy might be.

Remarkably, yet another official report (the fifth since the collapse) was commissioned. Sir John Chadwick, 67, a former lord justice of the Court of Appeal and an expert in banking and insurance, was appointed to decide who would get money and how much. The victims' total losses are estimated at between £4 billion and £5 billion. It was Chadwick's job to keep the cost to the exchequer, groaning by now under the weight of bank bail-outs, to a minimum.

Paul Braithwate, the voluble head of the campaigning Equitable Members Action Group, who had turned his campaign into a full-time job, was disgusted:

Amazingly, after eight years' struggle, we have 21,000 paid-up members and have never been stronger. This is because of deep-felt outrage at the hypocrisy of such humbug as 'Fairness is in our DNA' – a claim made by our prime minister. Those who've lost out simply can't understand why depositors with banks such as Royal Bank of Scotland and Icesave have been fully protected, yet Equitable's pensioners are left to swing. It seems that we, the victims, will have to intensify our political fight for justice.

Still the foot-dragging continued. Despite intense pressure, a new Treasury minister, Liam Byrne, repeated the standard line to the Commons in October 2009. He said that compensation would be confined to 'people who have suffered disproportionate impact arising from maladministration and resulting in injustice accepted by the government'. Chadwick's scheme, outlining who would receive compensation and how much, would not be ready until spring 2010. It was an extraordinary admission, that a scandal that stretched back to New Labour's first years in office could drag on unresolved into the run-up to the 2010 general election.

What kept the issue alive all those years was the sheer determination of the victims of the collapse. Equitable Life policyholders were not the usual bunch of unfortunate, powerless insurance victims let down by a provider. They included in their number some of the best educated, most articulate, most legally aware policyholders anywhere in the world. This was never a group that would take the loss to their savings lying down. They wanted action against the perpetrators of the debacle, and they held the government – in the shape of the FSA, the Government Actuaries Department and the Treasury – responsible for their plight. These agencies were in their view, and to use a New Labour phrase, not fit for purpose.

While regulatory failure dated back to the 1980s and the Tories, Tony Blair and Gordon Brown bore a lot of the responsibility for the poor and indulgent supervisory culture that had allowed Equitable to continue to function normally even when its problems were very apparent. Brown's belief that a single all-powerful City regulator could somehow correct the mistakes of the past proved to be a ghastly error. He believed that a change in architecture could be a substitute for better regulation. The new team at the FSA, headed by Davies, at times seemed as concerned about protecting its own reputation as dealing with the plight of policyholders, many of whose lives were being ruined by the experience.

Pressure on the government was ratcheted up in August 2008 when an angry and frustrated chairman of Equitable, Vanni Treves, added his voice to the cries for justice and restitution for stricken investors. With 30,000 policyholders having died since the society closed to new business, Treves was acutely aware of the urgency of the situation. 'More people are dying. We are going to lobby with all the vigour that we can to get the commission established quickly,' he said. It would be 'absolutely deplorable if the Parliamentary Ombudsman's coruscating conclusions' were not followed immediately, as this would question 'the credibility of the Ombudsman's office'.

Critics argued that taxpayers should not bear the burden of any payout; after all they had been forced to pour billions of pounds into keeping the banking system afloat. Treves responded that Equitable was 'genuinely unique' as it had not been properly regulated, and that a payout would not set a precedent for the public purse. 'It is a fact that policyholders paid through their premiums for the regulation which, in the event, turned out to be failing,' he said. He rejected any notion that the policyholders were all middle- and upper-income individuals who could afford to bear the loss:

Policyholders paid for their side of the bargain and the government should now pay for theirs. Policyholders were entitled to proper regulation and did not get it. Fifty per cent of policyholders were ordinary people – such as Tesco and Post

Office workers. They are spread all across the country. To pretend we are simply representing the issues of Middle England is not justified.

While Treves openly called for compensation, he would not be drawn on how much should be given to members:

Neither the society, nor the parliamentary ombudsman has at any time or any way suggested what the total compensation figure should be. We have not done so because it would be foolish or impertinent to try to do the work of the compensation commission.

He later pledged, 'If the government does not accept the parliamentary ombudsman's recommendations, then I will ask it what has happened to its moral compass. We will strain every muscle to bring this to a conclusion.'

Since 2001 Treves had operated with both his heart and his mind. As a hard-headed City lawyer and businessman he wanted to run Equitable on proper lines – but in a way that was best for the society's policyholders, many of whom had been damaged by the debacle. He believed he had managed to carry out both objectives:

We've compensated all those policyholders to whom we owed a debt and we've paid hundreds of thousands of people hundreds of millions of pounds through rectification and compensation schemes. So, we've done the right thing, we believe, as a society to our policyholders. We think it is high time that the government did the same.

The Equitable saga provides a graphic example of how long it takes to resolve a crisis in the financial services sector. The rundown strategy directed by Vanni Treves had come to end on 27 November 2008. Equitable was forced to call a halt to the sale of its remaining business – the £6 billion with-profits fund – after a year of trying to find a buyer. Poor market conditions as a result of the credit crunch were blamed, with a disappointed Treves pledging to focus on a stable and secure run-off of the society. In March 2009 chief executive Charles Thomson announced his departure after eight years at Equitable Life. His departure was not without controversy because of the high levels of remuneration he had received during his period as caretaker of the company, including a total compensation of almost £1 million in his final year.

By 2009 two-thirds of the policies that had been in force since 2000 had been cancelled. Of those remaining, the average pension pot for individuals stood at £48,000, with group schemes of £4,000 per member. One investor, 65-year-old Peter Hart from Dover, who had opened an Equitable plan in 1990, lost £125,000 after cashing his with-profit bonds in 2000. His pension had fallen from £34,000 a year to only £18,000. He told the *Sunday Times*:

> The effects of actual and anticipated losses have caused me to sell a large house and move to a smaller property. I had to postpone my retirement and generally cut back on expenditure, more or less on everything. Sadly, I recommended Equitable Life to several friends and, so far, two have died. There will be no justice for them.

Among others sharing the pain was fellow investor Rodger Watts, who had put £520,000 into an Equitable pension plan. Sometime later he began to receive letters from the society warning that it would have to cut heavily to meet its GAR payout obligations. Eventually, when he was able to take his money out, Watts found that his investment had fallen to £375,000.

He told the BBC News website in January 2009:

> I think the government owe me £317,000 – that's what I've lost in terms of the initial sum and the growth it failed to make.

That's a lot of money. I'd saved all my life – every penny. I'd put it in a pension, as you are advised to do. Now, because of maladministration and bad regulation I've lost all that money. When you work hard and save you don't expect that to happen through regulatory failure. It's the government's fault.

Another policyholder badly hit was Ann Berry from West Sussex. The mother of four retired as a physiotherapist in 1998, just ahead of her 60th birthday. While self-employed in the later stages of her career, Berry – by now divorced – held four separate personal pension plans. On retirement she was advised to consolidate them into an annuity with what seemed the best provider – Equitable Life.

With the possibility of living another 30 or more years, she decided to accept the society's suggestion that she take out a with-profits policy which would increase in value year on year and hopefully keep pace with inflation. An average bonus rate of 6.5 per cent was assumed. At this time Equitable was declaring bonuses of 10 per cent or more per annum.

When Berry retired her total pension pot with Equitable came to £110,000, which, after tax, initially brought her an income of £400 a month. By 2001 this had risen to £500 a month, but has since dropped back to around £400 – some £300 short of where Berry believed it would have been given Equitable's estimates in 1998. A career in the health service yields a small NHS pension, which when added to the state pension brings in just under £500 a month, plus income from a bond, currently providing another £260. She told me in 2009:

I first learned that Equitable had a potential problem in January 1999, when the society became involved in proceedings to gain approval for its GAR cuts. I first became seriously alarmed when listening to the *Today* programme on Radio 4 in December 2000 and heard John Humphrys announce that Equitable Life had closed its doors to further business.

In common with the vast majority of the Equitable Life membership, I continued to believe what we now know to be the disinformation put out by the Society and I voted in 2002 in favour of the Compromise Agreement, commonly known now as the *con*promise. For that is what it was: a con trick for which we were persuaded to sign up, on the assurance that it would put an end to the society's problems.

Even though Equitable attempted to apply crippling market-value adjustors to her policy, Berry fought the society and was eventually able to withdraw £25,000 without penalty, which she invested elsewhere. When she retired in 1998, she sold her house in Chichester and bought a three-bedroomed detached bungalow in nearby Selsey. But that too proved too costly in her straitened circumstances and in 2005 she downsized again, this time buying a two-bedroom bungalow with a small garden. She summed up:

The impact on my life has been considerable. I did not expect ever to enjoy a retirement of luxury, but I did believe I had planned for a retirement free from acute financial concerns, and one where I could afford to go on holiday abroad from time to time and also maintain a sufficiently large house in which to accommodate visiting family. I have four children, all of whom now have spouses and children, and we are a close family who enjoy visiting and spending time with each other. I now have nine grandchildren, ranging in age from 17 years down to ten-month-old twins.

The government's failure to supervise what went on at Equitable was a serious dereliction of duty. Initially it failed to appreciate the full scale of the coming crisis. Then it acted slowly and indecisively when collapse became inevitable, and allowed new victims to be caught up in the Equitable train crash. And when it all went wrong, the Labour government – which should have been alert to the best interests of savers and pensioners – turned its face against any kind of bailout or compensation, leaving more than a million hard-working and -saving policyholders high and dry.

The cost of a rescue would have been a fraction of the sums it eventually paid out to all and sundry when the credit crisis struck, including the unwise savers who trusted in the Icelandic banks which sunk beneath the cold Arctic waters. Indeed, had the problem been tackled in 1998 it would have cost a quarter of the current estimated bill: £1 billion rather than £4 billion. But Equitable Life policyholders were, in Labour's view, just another bunch of over-protected investors who now wanted the taxpayer to pick up the tab. Gordon Brown and his team, fixated on the potential fiscal commitment, were not going to lift a finger.

Pension experts have warned that, after a decade-long fight for justice, most Equitable policyholders will receive little or nothing. Ros Altmann, the former government pension adviser, is pessimistic: 'Nobody will get much from the government at all. Even now the victims do not know what help they might get, when they will get it or whether they will get anything at all.' Tens of thousands of the million-plus victims have already died waiting for justice. Most likely to receive compensation are those whose entire retirement savings were with the firm, those who lost most money and the elderly. Losers will be those who had money with other companies and those still young enough to work, giving them time to keep on saving.

Liberal Democrat spokesman Vince Cable is just one of those to have called for a fast-track compensation scheme to rectify what he has called 'festering injustice'. In his judgement the fiasco exposed the government at 'its most shabby and disreputable'.

CHAPTER 8

Dithering and disagreement

It was a bright early morning in May 1997 as Frank Field passed through the security cordon at the entrance to Downing Street and headed for his first Cabinet meeting. Days earlier New Labour's landslide victory in the general election had inspired a mood of euphoria in the country – Britain now had a young leader with energy and new ideas. To the surprise of many, one of these ideas had been to invite Field, a maverick on social issues, to reform the welfare system by 'thinking the unthinkable' – a role the experienced MP for Birkenhead intended to take very seriously indeed.

The brief Field had been given included responsibility for pensions. As he stepped inside Number 10 and mingled with other ministers still basking in the glow of election victory, Field's mind was crammed with schemes and initiatives. Here, he felt, was a new government with an agenda for change: the possibilities seemed endless and exciting.

But even then, Field knew that things would be problematic. For a start he was horribly aware that he and others had been kept in the dark over Brown's pension tax raid. 'I did not know anything about the £5 billion annual tax on pension funds until it had happened,' he said later.

When I saw the prime minister afterwards he was weighing up the consequences of the move. 'Gordon didn't tell me that,'

Blair revealed. You cannot imagine Mrs Thatcher allowing those sorts of mega-reforms going through without her making sure somebody explained to her what the consequences would be.

Then came the recognition that Number 11 had never been keen on Field's appointment. 'There was a dispute about the post from the start which should have suggested to me not to do the job,' Field admitted. 'I told the prime minister, "You will never be more powerful than you are today, and if you cannot make the appointments you want today it doesn't look good for the future."'

However, I thought being secretary of state was important and, of course, it was only later I realised that it didn't matter who you were. There was tension from the very beginning in government. Gordon Brown was all-powerful in the domestic sphere and very unyielding and ungenerous in his approach, which made governing very difficult. He was not prepared to listen to people and would avoid discussion and debate about a subject. If I wanted to see him about something, he would not deal directly with you – but, instead, would use an intermediary.

That first Cabinet meeting set the tone for all that followed. When it came to social issues, Gordon Brown and the Treasury clearly saw themselves as the only show in town. Field could 'think' about pensions all he liked; it was Brown who would have the final say on this and many other issues. He proposed to save on the public purse by making state pensions means tested, and add to government coffers by taxing private and company schemes. And that was that.

Field hotly contested Brown's view but found little support in Cabinet. Even Blair, who, it emerged, actually disagreed with Brown's vision on pensions, deferred to him. Worse was to follow. At the first meeting of the Cabinet's Welfare to Work subcommittee Field condemned Brown's proposed pension plan as unworkable. The discussion was terminated. Afterwards, Brown confronted Field. 'How could you disagree with me?' he asked. 'I thought you were my friend.' 'It's just because I am your friend that I could disagree with you,' replied Field, puzzled by the chancellor's fury.

The tragedy is that Field was prepared to do exactly what Blair had asked him to do – think the unthinkable. With a lifetime's experience of helping the poor, Field agreed passionately with Brown's principle of self-reliance, but was concerned with the way in which it would be implemented. In particular he pointed out that in a system whereby 46 million Britons would be entitled to at least one welfare benefit, large-scale fraud would be endemic. 'Your pension plans will create chaos,' Field told Brown.

Field's 'big idea' was to create a collective system independent of the state that would deliver to a coalition of people something they couldn't buy in the private market. He was on a mission to show that there were various ways a nation could make collective provision for old age. Among the key elements was a scheme on the lines of the Swedish model, in which all those not already in occupational pensions could be included. Field was concerned that a mass system of means testing, as proposed by Brown, would be an invitation to fraudulent claims.

'In an era when people are increasingly restive about taxation, we needed to convince them it was appropriate to make contributions which they didn't think of as taxes,' he told me in an interview at the Commons some 12 years later.

We are still trying to do that. Even now it's hard to push taxes above something like 34 per cent of GDP, but the government wants to spend 40 per cent – and there are various ways you can do this in the short run, one of which is to mount up the debt. But in the longer run surely the answer is to persuade people to save for their old age by guaranteeing them a pension that takes you above means test, so that everything you save is a bonus for you.

Field concluded:

My starting point was that I didn't think his [Brown's] plans would work, but as a member of a team I hoped time would deliver the reforms we needed. It was quite clear that Blair did not have the appetite to master a brief that would enable him to impose his will on the chancellor. Eventually, after 18 months, he got tired of the confrontations in Cabinet with me arguing with Gordon, so he suggested moving me in a reshuffle, which I declined.

Not surprisingly Field's stay as a minister proved short-lived. When he found that he was consistently receiving no support in Cabinet for his radical proposals he felt after a year that he had little choice but to resign. But he hung on in office until October 1998. Field believes that Blair effectively backed Brown for one of two reasons: 'Either Blair had ceded domestic issues to Brown [as many have long suspected had occurred as part of the Granita restaurant pact over the Labour leadership after the death of John Smith]. Or, he simply didn't want the constant ear-bashing he was getting from Brown on these issues. So he gave in.'

The Frank Field episode, exposing the deep divisions between Numbers 10 and 11 Downing Street, goes a long way to explaining the pensions disarray that followed. Blair wanted to see some new ideas, but Brown was determined to protect what he saw as his turf. Blair felt that pensions were an issue that needed to be addressed, but Brown didn't regard them as a major priority and didn't fully engage with the issues they threw up. The net result was an approach that involved disagreement and tinkering at best, and muddle and inaction at worst.

As minister of welfare reform from 1997 to 1998, Field turned out to be the first of ten Cabinet ministers, spanning 13 years of government, to be given responsibility for pensions. After Field resigned, his responsibilities were taken on by Harriet Harman who, as social services secretary 1998–2001, also took charge of pensions. In 2001 New Labour created the office of pensions secretary and its occupants were: Alistair Darling (2001–2), Andrew Smith (2002–4), Alan Johnson (2004–5), David Blunkett (2005), John Hutton (2005–7), Peter Hain (2007–8), James Purnell (2008–9) and from June 2009 Yvette Cooper. There were even more pension ministers, some 17 at the last count. These startling figures further demonstrate both how little concern there was for continuity and how little importance was attached to a key area of public policy.

Labour had promised joined-up government. When it came to pensions it managed to achieve almost the opposite. The department responsible for pensions would pour out policy documents on a regular basis. The Treasury would then shoot them down or undermine them. It was prepared to find money for the NHS, education and bailing out the banking system, but the needs of the elderly, from long term health care to retirement, were not on its radar.

Several episodes illustrate New Labour's disjointed and constantly shifting approach to retirement provision. In 2002, five years after coming to office, the government undertook one of its more rational pension initiatives when it attempted to simplify the ferociously complicated tax system that surrounded them. In a Green Paper published in December Pensions Secretary Andrew Smith proposed replacing the eight existing tax regimes with one. Individuals would be able to accumulate a lifetime pension pot of £1.4 million tax-free with a maximum £200,000 a year contributed. Any pension pot above these limits would lose the tax breaks for savers contributing to a pension. At the time the £1.4 million limit was seen as reasonably generous. It would provide an annual retirement income estimated at between £60,000 and £65,000, well above the average.

The Inland Revenue calculated that this plan would only affect 5,000 people with pension pots above the limit. There was nevertheless fierce opposition from business leaders. Labour sympathisers, including Niall FitzGerald, then joint chairman of the conglomerate Unilever, and other senior figures from industry, lobbied Downing Street. Their argument was that the plan hit highly paid and valued staff. If the ceiling of £1.4 million was not raised, companies would only be able to hang on to vital staff by transferring them abroad.

Writing in the *Financial Times* on 8 September 2003 FitzGerald asserted:

We need to rebuild the position of strength the UK once enjoyed in company pension provision . . . the plan for a £1.4 million limit on the accumulated value of pensions is another example of a failure to see the arguments through to their conclusion. This surtax on saving will add further cost and complexity to business.

By the following March the National Audit Office was reporting that, in fact, 10,000 people would be affected by the plan. New Labour caved in, and the chancellor duly announced in his Budget an immediate limit of £1.5 million, rising to £1.8 million by 2010, with implementation delayed until 2006.

The policy of radical tax simplification nevertheless remained intact, and it drew widespread applause. The financial services industry moved to take advantage of it by developing a new product – the Self-Invested Pension Plan (SIPP) – which allowed clients to make better use of the tax-free limit.

But by the spring of 2009, after the credit crisis had taken its toll, Labour was seeking to claw back the new favourable regime for pension savings. A row over the size of the pension of Royal Bank of Scotland chief Sir Fred Goodwin drew attention to the fact that high earners were sheltering income in retirement funds. Chancellor Alistair Darling felt that the well-off sections of society, including bankers and company directors, were being treated too generously by the tax regime.

In a populist move aimed at City fat cats and the bonus culture he removed tax relief for higher-income taxpayers – those earning more than £150,000 a year – paying into pension funds. He sought to explain the change by saying he was introducing more fairness into the tax system. The reality was a Labour government taking back what it had given in recognition of the ruin which the financial community had brought down on the rest of the country.

The move undermined the quest for simplicity that had been proposed by Andrew Smith and implemented by Brown just three years earlier. One senior Whitehall official remarked that the move was 'gratuitous' and entirely political. Tom McPhail, head of pension research at respected investment advisers Hargreaves Landsdown, argued that the government was 'using a sledge-hammer to crack a nut' and accused Labour of again messing with the stability which long-term pension investors required.

A second episode demonstrates even more strongly how New Labour could spot an important issue, look as though it was going to address it and then drop the ball. This time the pensions secretary involved was Alan Johnson, who in the lead-up to the general election of 2005 was given the delicate task by Blair of reshaping the pensions of public-sector workers.

Blair's initiative stemmed from the findings of the three-person Pensions Commission he had set up in 2002 to look at the whole area of non-state pensions. The commission, the subject of a fierce dispute with Gordon Brown, was headed up by the cerebral former director general of the CBI Lord (Adair) Turner, its other members being Professor John Hills of the LSE and trade unionist Jeannie Drake. Among other things, they had identified public-sector pensions as an area that needed to be addressed.

Even to consider reforming pension provision for the strongly unionised public sector was a brave move. Blair had, however, already shown himself to be prepared to take on the unions,

Labour's traditional allies, in the party reforms that had helped pave the way to his resounding 1997 election victory. He knew that in an era when pensions were struggling, tough decisions would have to be made about gold-plated public-sector provision.

Johnson seemed the ideal person for the task. With his slicked-back greying hair and liking for boxy suits with narrow lapels he gave the impression of being down to earth, and he had a winning, easy manner. What's more, he was one of the few working-class people in Blair's Cabinet, with the kind of aspirational personal history all too rare in New Labour. Born in London in 1950, he was orphaned at 12 and brought up by his older sister. On leaving grammar school at 15, he worked in various jobs before becoming a postman three years later. From there he rose within the union movement, becoming a branch official with the Communication Workers Union, later taking up a full-time post and becoming general secretary in 1993. Then he began his ascent through the Labour ranks. He became MP for Hull West and Hessle in 1997 and filled various ministerial positions before in 2004 becoming the first trade union official to join the Cabinet since the legendary Frank Cousins in 1964.

In the event, his union background didn't help him. When talks began in March 2005 he tried to persuade the public-sector unions to agree to an increase in the normal pension age from 60 to 65. This, he pointed out, would simply mirror the trend in the private sector. But the unions were bitterly opposed and talks broke off.

After the 2005 election Johnson resumed the negotiations from his new Cabinet seat at the Department of Trade and Industry with David Blunkett as the fifth pensions secretary. But Johnson came up against the big battalions at the TUC's annual conference in Brighton. In a major revolt, 13 different unions representing more than three million public-sector workers announced boldly that they were prepared to strike over the issue. As far as they were concerned, the retirement age of 60 – fought for by the labour movement over the generations – was sacrosanct. Moreover, the unions pointed out, they had helped to propel Labour to power in successive general elections. They were not going to be bullied into submission. The biggest wave of industrial action since the General Strike of 1926 was threatened if the government pressed ahead with its plans.

Faced with such mass dissent – and with Downing Street in full retreat – Johnson surrendered on 18 October 2005. The proposal that from 2013 the retirement age be lifted to 65 for existing public-sector workers in the Civil Service, health and education schemes was dropped. Instead, current workers could retire at 60, while new recruits would have to accept retirement at 65. Minor adjustments to the way in which future public-sector pension rights would be calculated – moving towards an average salary, instead of final salary approach – were agreed.

The TUC called this a 'sensible compromise', while Johnson talked up the deal, labelling it a 'breakthrough'. But this was New Labour spin. The government had been outmanoeuvred. Moreover, the TUC extracted a pledge from the government that new schemes would be earnings and index linked, thus protecting them against inflation. Retirement at 60 would still be an option if future staff funded an earlier retirement date by making larger contributions to the scheme.

All politics involves tactical retreats, but this was a full-scale strategic defeat. Yet again it showed muddled policy and an inability to see things through. What's more, it brought into sharp relief Labour's extraordinary double standard on pensions. Final salary schemes in the private sector had been virtually destroyed by constant government meddling and the 1997 tax raid. In the state sector Brown was still fighting against restoration of the earnings link for the universal state pension, a link that would have helped the poorest sections of society. Yet Johnson had managed to squeeze only the narrowest of concessions out of the unions and had even conceded the earnings link, something that the Treasury was resisting everywhere else.

Not surprisingly, the private sector was furious, claiming that the government had caved in to union pressure and set a bad – and unequally applied – precedent. The British Chambers of Commerce, representing small and medium-sized firms across the land, was forthright in its condemnation:

This deal is unacceptable from the standpoint of British business. The government needed to grasp the nettle and increase the public-sector retirement age for existing employees. They have failed to do this.

The early years of the new millennium were strewn with such uncertain or muddled moves, some sponsored by Blair, some by Brown, most undermined somewhere along the line. Two initiatives – the stakeholder pension and pensions credit – even managed to contradict each other. The irony here was that they both came from the same man: Gordon Brown.

The idea of the stakeholder was first popularised by journalist-turned-think-tank-chief Will Hutton in his 1995 book *The State We're In*. It had a ringing, socially inclusive sound to it, so it is scarcely surprising that it appealed to Blair. Critics were rather less impressed: they weren't quite clear what it all meant, other than that a stakeholder pension was supposed to be a low-cost, easy-to-purchase plan for people on below-average incomes. They had a suspicion that it wasn't much more than a bit of New Labour flag-waving jargon.

The task of putting some flesh on the bones was passed to Ron Sandler, a reforming former chief executive of Lloyd's of London insurance market. Later, in 2008, he would be the man to take on the role of chairman of a nationalised Northern Rock. His pedigree was impressive. Born in Bulawayo, Zimbabwe (then Southern Rhodesia) in 1952, he gained a degree in engineering from Queens' College, Cambridge and an MBA from Stanford University. He then moved into the City, where he was chief executive at Lloyd's from 1995 until

1999. After his skilful handing of the problems of the insurance market he was called in by the board of NatWest bank in 1999 as chief operating officer when it came under threat of takeover. He resigned after it fell prey to the acquisitive Royal Bank of Scotland. He moved on to become non-executive chairman of Computacenter.

In June 2001 Sandler was asked by Brown to carry out a review of the medium- and long-term retail savings industry, the aim being to plug the estimated £28 billion savings gap. Sandler identified two key problems: consumers were not getting value for money from savings and investment products, and the less well off were not putting enough aside in savings. He suggested that there were three principal causes. The complex nature of most financial products meant it was impossible for savers to know what they were being charged. Investors were over-reliant on advisers, whose advice could too easily be compromised by the commission they received from the creators of the products. And the cost of regulating products was pricing many out of the market.

Sandler's 'big idea' was to create a suite of basic, simple stakeholder investment products, including a pension, for those on lower salaries. They would be so reliable that those buying them would not need detailed explanations and financial advice. They would be cheap to set up because there would be no need to incur the usual expense of getting insurers or other financial institutions to verify that a particular product was suitable for the purchaser. They would also be so simple to set up and run that the industry could make them profitable.

Ruth Kelly, then financial secretary to the Treasury, embraced Sandler's findings:

> This report sets out a vision of a simpler, more transparent and more competitive medium- and long-term savings industry which the government endorses. Ron Sandler's recommendations have the potential to benefit consumers, the retail investment industry and improve the workings of the market.

Unfortunately, when it actually came to implementing the new pension things started to unravel. Few financial service providers wanted to market it when the commission fees on offer were so low. They also feared that if they sold such schemes to lower-income groups they might well get caught up in accusations of mis-selling. In addition, there was real concern that in the rush to simplify, investor protection was being reduced to an absolute minimum. Consumer watchdog groups and the Financial Services Authority feared that unsophisticated individuals would be ripped off or would buy inappropriate products.

Lord Turner, who became chairman of the Financial Services Authority in the autumn of 2008, was not surprised it didn't work:

> First, it was not really possible to design a sort of light touch, safe harbour regime when you are selling this [stakeholder pension]. You have to go through all the processes. That turned out to be very, very difficult to do.
>
> Secondly, the price cap (the suggested half a percentage point ceiling on management charges) meant that industry looked at this and said I can't make money out of somebody on £15,000 or £20,000 per annum. The administration costs work when you are selling to someone at £50,000 a year, but don't work at £20,000 a year because the revenue does not equal the cost. They became quite popular among higher-income people because they were price capped, but the industry made almost no attempt to sell these to lower-income people.
>
> Finally, you had to nominate a stakeholder provider. But it turned out that 80 per cent of the nominated schemes had no members in them. These things were just shells.

There was another problem too. Back in September 2000 – in other words before work began on the stakeholder idea – Brown had outlined plans at the annual Labour Party conference for what he labelled the Pension Credit. This had begun life as the Minimum

Income Guarantee (MIG) for every retiree, by which the nation's poorest pensioners would receive an increment above the basic pension, raised in line with earnings. Brown then announced that the MIG was to be reformed in favour of a Savings Credit. The big change, aside from the name, was that because the new credit was deemed to be 'savings friendly' it could be claimed by people who had already put money aside for a modest private pension. Within a year the Savings Credit had metamorphosed – into the Pension Credit, by which some three million pensioners were given a means-tested guaranteed minimum income.

There were difficulties with the scheme from the start. Apart from anything else, the credit proved fiendishly difficult to claim because the form filling involved was so complex. Frank Field, for one, was dubious. 'The chancellor has directed more taxpayers' money to the poorest pensioners than any of his predecessors for 50 years,' he stated in an interview for this book in 2009:

But even here his policy is destructive in the longer term because Pension Credit is means tested. The most carefully costed alternative strategy was put forward by the Pensions Reform Group, which I chair. Here was a scheme that put a shelf life on to Pension Credit by building up capital to fund everyone a minimum pension. Such a guaranteed minimum pension can be secured only if the whole of society pools the risks of delivering such an outcome. It is a collective, but non-state-led reform. The proposal was never seriously considered.

Whatever the rights and wrongs of the Pension Credit may have been, perhaps its most glaring shortcoming was that by the time it was implemented in 2003 it clearly conflicted with Brown's stakeholder initiative. Low earners were being encouraged to invest in a stakeholder pension, but it looked as though most of them would actually be better off going for the Pension Credit scheme. In fact, experts estimated that because the Pension Credit was really quite generous, a stakeholder pension only made sense to people earning at least £30,000 a year. It was, in other words, the best option for those for whom it was never intended.

And while all this was going on, yet another report was commissioned. This time it was the turn of Alistair Darling, the government's third pensions secretary, to seek outside advice. Known as a safe pair of hands who could be trusted with a complex and politically sensitive brief, Darling opted to ask the vastly experienced Alan Pickering, a leading pensions industry practitioner, to suggest better ways of delivering pensions. A partner with actuaries Watson Wyatt, Pickering was a member of the Occupational Pensions Board from 1991 to 1997, serving at one point as its deputy chairman. He was also chairman of the National Association of Pension Funds from 1999 to 2001 and later chairman of the European Federation for Retirement Provision (EFRP).

Pickering's report *A Simpler Way to Better Pensions* was published on 11 July 2002. The former NAPF chief did his best to ensure that his was a non-partisan document which did not fall foul of the Brown–Blair divide and could command support from opposition parties. Among those consulted were Tories David Willetts and Peter Lilley. 'The political buy-in has been critical in our desire to obtain input from the wider community,' Pickering stated in the foreword to his distinctive report in pink covers.

He concluded that the onus for saving had swung too far from individuals to employers. As a result, firms were proving increasingly unwilling to provide schemes and play their part in filling the UK's savings gap. Instead, they were closing final salary schemes.

Pickering's findings, written in the dry style one might expect from someone of his background, argued that measures had to be introduced to make it easier and cheaper for firms to keep final salary schemes going.

As well as his concern for occupational schemes, Pickering also called for the abolition of the minimum funding requirement and the guaranteed minimum pension, and he wanted a new, more powerful pensions regulator to replace the Occupational Pensions Regulatory Authority. In addition he disputed the need for survivors' pension rights. Over the years occupational pension plans had been encouraged by the regulator to make additional provision for the spouses/partners of deceased members so that pension rights did not die with them. In an age when most couples consisted of two working people Pickering felt this was an unnecessary luxury. Many of these points were later incorporated in a Government Green Paper.

There were other recommendations too. Pickering wanted to reduce the number of pension products to make them more user-friendly. He wanted to see a system by which people could transfer small amounts of pension entitlements accumulated at different employers into a single 'safe harbour' product. He proposed that multi-employer schemes be encouraged so that smaller firms could keep final salary schemes going. And he wanted simpler, more unified legislation.

Taken individually, there were some really good ideas here. The problem was that they did not build into a new pension strategy radical enough to deal with all the problems facing older people, currently and into the future. The pension consultant Ros Altmann was among those to criticise the report for not being bold enough. 'The Pickering Report does not really go the whole way in identifying all the inconsistencies and complications of the UK pension landscape,' she said. 'There are many more areas that need to be highlighted, but the report has not mentioned them, or has left them to other reviews.'

New Labour, though, did have one more stab at the pensions issue. This time the result was a seismic shock.

CHAPTER 9

Lord Turner plays the long game

The ink was barely dry on Sandler and Pickering when the prime minister made one final push for a radical solution to the pension crisis. It was clear that the cool reception to the stakeholder pension, the over-complicated Pension Credit and Pickering's low-key changes were not going to result in a safe retirement system. On 17 December 2002 Downing Street therefore set up the independent Pensions Commission under Lord Turner to examine the case for moving beyond voluntarism to compulsory pensions. Having failed to stamp his authority on pension reform through Frank Field, Blair was determined, amid the myriad of piecemeal reforms, to have one more go at more fundamental reforms.

Turner, then working at City investment bankers Merrill Lynch, was first sounded out by Downing Street adviser Geoff Mulgan, a key New Labour thinker. Having indicated his willingness to take up the cudgels, Turner received a call from Pensions Secretary Andrew Smith, who essentially confirmed that this was Blair's project.

Turner had an impressive background for the job. Born in Ipswich in October 1955, though growing up in Crawley and East Kilbride, he was educated initially at Hutchesons' Grammar School and then Glenalmond College. After leaving school, he went up to Gonville and Caius College, Cambridge, where he took a double first in history and economics before joining McKinsey & Company, where he became a director in 1982. Thirteen years later he was plucked from McKinsey, like his predecessor Sir Howard Davies, to be director general of the Confederation of British Industry, holding the job – straddling the decline of John Major's government and the first dizzy years of New Labour – until 1999. Like Davies, but by a very different route, he would end up as chairman of the Financial Services Authority in 2008.

The initial terms of reference for his commission support the notion that this was very much a Blair project. Turner was asked 'to review the adequacy of private pension saving in the UK, and advise on appropriate policy changes, including whether there was a need to move beyond the voluntary approach'. Significantly, there was no reference to the state sector – the chancellor's territory.

Turner and his co-commissioners Jeannie Drake, deputy general secretary of the Communications Workers Union, and John Hills, professor of social policy at the London School of Economics, concluded very quickly, however, that like it or not state pensions would have to be included. 'You had to consider the implications of the state for incentives created for private saving,' Turner told me in the summer of 2009. 'Blair from the beginning wanted to do something radical. He wanted a vision of where he was going with pensions. Gordon's basic gut feeling was, "No, we don't need to do anything too radical, I can do things to offset poverty via the tax credit" – the Treasury's own invention.'

Turner pressed on regardless. 'It was quite clear that you had to have an underpinning of a sort, a base load of the basic state pension which is as un-means tested as possible,' he said. Indeed, with the benefit of hindsight and without the political constraints he felt, Turner wishes he had gone further:

> If I were to rewrite the report I would have been more radical. I would probably have gone for increasing the state pension age more rapidly than we recommended so as to shift more people out of means testing. You want to get to the stage where there is a basic state pension that you can live on. Not a good life – but one that at least meets the definition of poverty.

Turner's technocratic background, notably his keen under-standing of data (a vital tool at McKinsey), and the political instincts he had honed at the CBI gave him the right credentials for finding a way forward for Britain's pensions. He was keen on the task ahead. The choice of other commission members also was shrewd. There was no way proposals on such an important issue were ever going to go anywhere without trade union participation – hence the choice of Drake, who at the time was also president of the TUC. She would prove critical to Turner when it came to selling a series of later retirement dates to the unions. Hills provided the commission's intellectual ballast.

The first or interim report in October 2004, with its shiny blue and turquoise cover, was a massive piece of work stretching to 316 pages with 212 pages of appendices. It included an enormous amount of demographic data, case studies from Britain and around the world, an extensive bibliography as well as a glossary explaining much of the technical gobbledegook beloved of pension experts.

I have to confess that when I first read it I was rather surprised to find how little space was given to Brown's 1997 tax raid and its implications. There was no attempt to calculate its financial impact. Instead, the report matter-of-factly noted that 'the actions of the Government (in 1986 and 1997) and of employers were predicated on the assumptions of long-term returns which were over-optimistic'.

Turner did note, however, that the Civil Service had consistently and completely overestimated the amount of money going into private-sector pensions. This in turn had bred a sense of com-placency about the impending retirement crisis. 'They were wrong by tens of billions of pounds, a couple of per cent of GDP,' Turner told me. In one case uncovered by the commission, Barclays Global Investors – the asset management arm of Barclays, sold to Black Rock in New York in 2009 – had changed the status of one of its companies. 'This produced some figure of multi-billions of apparent private savings, which of course it wasn't. The figures were completely screwed up,' he observed.

Turner and his team were politically savvy. They were not prepared to allow the headlines and analysis in the following day's newspapers to be stolen by the historic debate over who was ultimately responsible for the destruction of final salary pensions. To have done so would have made an immediate enemy of Brown and the Treasury, who Turner needed on side if his proposed reforms were to have any chance of success. He would have enough problems convincing Brown and the Treasury that it was time to restore the earnings link for the universal state pension – an expensive proposition – and to bring an end to the large-scale means testing of the Pension Credit.

The interim report revealed that Turner believed the existing system was completely unsustainable. In his view the solution lay in a mix of higher taxes, a later retirement age and higher semi-enforced savings. The report team found that population trends suggested that neither an increasing birth rate nor continuous excess immigration and settlement would provide an answer to the problems posed by an ageing population. Population growth would actually make the long-term problem even worse. Turner's two main proposals were stark: the state pension age should rise in line with life expectancy, and official retirement ages in both the public and private sectors should be deferred. The report concluded that a 'rise in the average rate of retirement was inevitable'. It looked at a number of scenarios and made the case, in the first instance, for lifting the male retirement age to 66 years. But this was not a recommendation.

These proposals were entirely logical given Turner's reassessment of increasing life expectancy in the UK, but they represented a reversal of years of thinking about old age. Since the Second World War the British public has come to assume that advances in technology and economic growth mean earlier and earlier retirement and more leisure. For their part, many employers welcome the retirement of an older worker. They know that a younger person will command a lower salary. They also sometimes feel that those starting out have more energy and creativity than those who have been around for a while, who may have lost their motivation and be grimly hanging on to a job purely for the salary.

What's more, early retirement has been built into one huge area of the employment market – the public sector – for years. Five million workers in Britain have embarked on careers assuming that they will retire at 60. On the surface this seems a strange anomaly. The original rationale, though, was that some sort of reward for public service was only fair when average wages in the private sector outstripped those in public service by leaps and bounds.

Earlier retirement, then, had become a watchword of late-twentieth-century Britain. And now Turner was saying precisely the opposite. Everyone would be affected by his plans, public-sector workers in particular, whose retirement age seemed even more out of kilter in an era when their remuneration had improved markedly. (Indeed one of the impacts of the credit crunch and the subsequent recession and flirtation with deflation – falling prices and wages – has been that average pay in the public sector has actually moved ahead of that in the private sector.) Turner realised that among the many battles to be fought was one with the unions, who would have to persuaded to forgo their advocacy of earlier retirement.

'It was a very sensitive issue for Jeannie Drake,' Turner revealed during his conversations with me in 2009. 'The state pension age becomes sort of inconographic in the trade union movement. But Jeannie could see, first of all, there was long-term logic in it, and that second, there was absolutely no way that we were going to get the basic state pension back linked to average earnings, to stop its decline in value, unless the flip side was a long-term rise in the state pension age.'

What was proposed in the second and final Turner Report – released on 30 November 2005 – was that in the state sector the pension age for men and women would rise gradually: from 65 to 66 from 2024, to 67 from 2034, and to 68 from 2044. Everyone under the age of 47 in 2005 would therefore be affected. Interestingly, the Conservatives were to go even further. In October 2009 Shadow Chancellor George Osborne outlined plans to lift the retirement age for men to 66 by 2016, eight years ahead of Labour. The retirement age for women would be lifted to 65 by 2020. Osborne vowed to 'hold the review which the Turner Report itself proposed and which the government has never held'.

Turner's second big idea was that from 2010 the basic state pension should return to being linked with average earnings rather than prices. This of course went directly against Brown's own views on the subject. Brown believed that his own reform to pensions, the means-tested Pension Credit, satisfactorily dealt with the problem of a very basic state pension. Turner, by contrast, felt that linking the basic state pension to average earnings from 2010 would help reduce poverty and render unnecessary Brown's cumbersome pensions credit with its bureaucratic and complicated system of means testing.

There was also another key idea in the report, which received rather less attention at the time. Turner proposed creating a National Pensions Saving Scheme (NPSS), in which all employees without existing occupational schemes would be enrolled. This, he felt, was vital if Britain was to cope in the future with an ageing population. If people on lower incomes could be made to sign up to the new scheme, then the state pension would become ever less significant, except for a small minority at the bottom end of the income scale. Initially the NPSS was nicknamed BritSave in the media. Subsequently and during the planning process it became known as the Personal Account (PA). In January 2010 it was rebranded again, as the National Employment Savings Trust (NEST).

Other important proposals included making the state pension based on UK residency and not on contributions, and making the state second pension – for people who had paid higher National

Insurance contributions and not joined an occupational scheme – a flat-rate payment.

Turner was heading for trouble. The Treasury did not want a 'big reform.' It was quite happy with its usual policy of muddling through. And there was certainly no way that Brown would accept Turner's proposal to restore the link between pensions and earnings.

At a private lunch held at One Aldwych, one of London's trendy minimalist hotels, shortly before the release of his report, Turner – who rarely shows passion in public – was incandescent. In October 2005 Alan Johnson had given into demands that the retirement date for public-sector workers be held at 60. Turner feared that the deal for the public sector would make it harder for him to sell a later retirement age to the other unions and the rest of the workforce. With his final recommendations pending, including an eventual rise in the state pension age to 68 years, he felt the soft treatment for public-sector workers might undermine his case and the political momentum.

Worse was to come. On 24 November 2005, six days before the Pensions Commission report was due to be published, the *Financial Times* printed leaked extracts of a letter written by Brown to Turner stating that the report's author should not assume the Pension Credit link to average earnings would continue beyond 2008. It was a highly technical point but crucial to Turner's calculations.

If the money to maintain the earnings link for the Pension Credit was not there, then the whole basis of Turner's reforms, which envisaged extending the earnings link to all basic state pension, was undermined. The leaked letter left the impression that if Turner's proposals were to be implemented the only way they could be financed was through a tax increase. It looked like a deliberate attempt at sabotaging the proposals and, if it was, demonstrated the lengths that Brown was willing to go to maintain his hegemony over the domestic agenda.

Suddenly, pension reform was front-page news, portrayed by

media political editors as the latest episode in the turf war between Number 10 and the Treasury. Michael White and Patrick Wintour, writing in the *Guardian*, summed up Turner's predicament:

> In addressing the pension crisis, Lord Turner has faced the biggest intellectual challenge of his career, looking to find a consensus on one of the most technical and politically charged issues facing the country. It has meant working with three ministers, trying to decipher what an only semi-cooperative Treasury will wear.

Turner decided to press on. He knew that Brown was against him – that he feared the expense the Turner proposals would entail and that he felt the status quo could be make to work, albeit with possible adjustments. But Turner calculated that he had the backing of Blair and prime ministerial aide Matthew Taylor. The PM – who had after all initiated the Pensions Commission in the first place – might well regard the changes proposed as unwelcome because they posed political difficulties, but he also accepted that a radical rethink was nevertheless necessary.

The Brown intervention clearly disturbed the commission members. But Turner recalls that they decided to stick to their guns and press ahead without trimming their far-reaching proposals. Turner, Jeannie Drake and John Hills jointly decided: 'We are going to stick to the logic of what we are saying. It is the role of an independent commission to say of course there will be political debate and press commentary. But we have to stick to what we are saying.'

Turner therefore went ahead and published his report. Like its interim predecessor, it was accompanied by a weighty volume of appendices, this time running to 304 pages. It was what had been asked for: an ambitious, far-reaching plan designed to deliver a respectable income for those retiring in the ensuing 45 years.

Whatever criticisms can be made of the report – and it certainly has failings (see Chapter 10) – to its credit it had the courage to deal with a series of truths that the government had been ducking. First and foremost it recognised that in a period when people are living ever longer, sticking with the status quo is not an option. On average, life expectancy in Britain is now 80 for women and 75 for men – thanks to medical advances, better health care and diet, and more exercise. Moreover, by 2050 there will be far fewer young people around to provide the nation with its wealth. So ensuring that there is adequate provision for the swelling numbers of pensioners represents a growing challenge.

It has to be recognised too that with longer life expectancy come higher expectations. The baby boomer generation – those born between 1945 and 1960 – are revolutionising what it means to be old because their attitudes are so different to those of their parents. Market research shows they are aspirant, demanding and imaginative consumers of both products and services, seeking out information, using the Internet and refusing to be defined by their age group. Even before the bulk of the boomers retire, the lingering stereotypes of the average senior citizen as a frail and passive creature are out of date. Innovations like the Freedom Pass in London mean that they are far from being housebound and can travel widely to pursue paid work, voluntary activities and leisure passions.

Michael O'Higgins, Audit Commission chairman, commented in 2008, 'By 2029 nearly 40 per cent of England's population will be over 50. These are active people, anxious to stay independent as long as possible. Ex-punk rockers and Rolling Stones fans are not going to be happy with a cup of tea and daytime TV.' The current generation of over-60s is the healthiest and most active on record, and the increasing number of retirees has led to an explosion in leisure-based markets. For some retirement is an opportunity to concentrate on staying young.

It seems that the older we get as a society, the harder we all try to appear youthful. Cosmetic surgery and other anti-ageing procedures like Botox are booming. Figures show that Britons are spending £225 million a year on such treatments, around half of which are undergone in the attempt to look younger. The divorced or widowed are busy forming or developing relationships, and dating websites for the over-50s – the so-called later love market – are big business.

Many retirees keen on excitement and adventure, and now with plenty of leisure time, take up extreme hobbies and go on exotic holidays. Taking up a mainstream sport appeals to many – to help them keep fit and mentally alert. On weekdays suburban golf courses and clubhouses are busy, while there has been significant growth in activities, such as swimming, yoga and dance classes, which offer social and health benefits to seniors.

With their considerable financial power and the prospect of decades of healthy life ahead, those in their sixties and seventies are exerting a powerful influence on our culture. Archaeology, studies of family trees, amateur astronomy, history and many other reflective activities have all received major boosts as more retirees seek stimulation. Self-improvement through adult learning groups and colleges is also popular. Up to 40 years ago this was not a realistic option for most retired people, for whom access to education was limited. But since the 1960s colleges, home-based courses and even a special university entirely for those of the 'third age' have started up.

Given a little effort, it is now easier for pensioners to learn than at any time before, and in England alone there are officially more than 600,000 learners over the age of 60. The Open University, birthplace of modern home study and Labour Prime Minister Harold Wilson's greatest legacy, now takes 3 per cent of its students from among the over-65s and 6 per cent from the 55–64 age group. Among my former colleagues one senior editor retired early to pursue his passion for military history through the Open University. Another acquaintance, who originally went straight from school into the law and regrets that his formal education was cut short, made up for the lost university experience by pursuing a masters degree in war studies at Kings College, London.

Volunteering is also popular with many people looking for a change after a lifetime of paid employment. Figures show that 35 per cent of people aged 75-plus regularly give up some of their free time to help others. Participation in society in other ways, such as joining pressure groups and forums, is also high among current retirees.

Some of the biggest changes to cater for those over-60s enjoying their new-found leisure are to be found in housing. American-style condominiums have cropped up all over the UK and offer a range of facilities from laundry and cleaning services, restaurants and bars to sports like tennis, bowls and croquet, plus libraries and other facilities for self-improvement.

Evidence of the increasing importance and influence of the senior – or 'grey pound' – market is the increasing attention from the advertising industry. Traditionally neglected by ad agencies and their clients, with 20 million consumers in this bracket holding 80 per cent of the nation's wealth the situation is changing fast. Statistics tell advertisers that over-50s buy 80 per cent of top-of-the-range cars, 50 per cent of skincare products and 80 per cent of leisure cruises, while over the past two decades consumption by Europe's over-50s has risen three times as fast as that of the rest of the population.

Inevitably, alongside greater expectations come elements of greater dependency. If many aspects of modern retirement are positive, there has been one significant downside – the problem of long-term care costs for families. Middle-aged couples – many already stuck with the spiralling costs of children living at home – are having to pay more for care of parents as they live longer and their pensions and savings fall short. The figures are frightening for the 150,000 elderly who have to pay for long-term care. The average annual care bill is nearly £18,000, while the average income is £6,650, leaving the elderly or their families over £11,300 a year to find from savings.

Half a million people are in residential care and a third of these are required to pay all or most of the bill themselves. Care funding is subject to a strict means test. In England and Wales anyone with assets of £13,000 to £22,250 is expected to pay in part. Those assessed as having assets of more than that must pay their own care bills in full. This means that muddling through is becoming increasingly less of an option when it comes to making provision for old age. One simple statistic makes this crystal clear: by 2050 there will be 16.2 million people in Britain of pensionable age. Turner recognised this, expressed it in unambiguous terms and voiced a coherent plan for accommodating it.

Gordon Brown was looking at a different set of figures. The implication of the Turner Report was that the cost of state pension provision would have to jump from 6.4 per cent of national income to between 7.5 per cent and 8 per cent by 2045 (figures still lower, though, than those that prevail in such EU members as Germany). Turner's way of coping with the additional cost was, of course, to roll back the retirement age. The first group to be affected would be women, who have traditionally retired earlier than men. After that the pensionable age would rise to 66 by 2030, to 67 by 2040 and to 68 by 2050.

The minister who found himself in the hot seat as Brown girded his loins to do battle with Turner was John Hutton, the sixth Labour cabinet secretary to have pensions as his brief. An Oxford-educated intellectual with expertise in industrial policy, he found himself in a situation that was now becoming depressingly familiar. As he explained to me in an interview in late 2009:

The tensions were in the beginning, in my view, between Gordon and Tony about how the Treasury and Number 10 looked at the Department of Work and Pensions. I think the Treasury wanted to own it lock, stock and barrel. I think Number 10, not unreasonably – because it is where the prime minister is – wanted to have a sort of reasonable grip on it. I think gradually over the years Tony got more of handle of what was going on in the DWP than early in his premiership.

Hutton agreed with Turner and Blair on the reforms required, but Brown did not make it easy. As chancellor of the exchequer he staged a very public fight over the cost of restoring the earnings link for state pensions. As we have seen, vital correspondence on the issue was leaked to the press. For a while it looked as though the whole project would be allowed to die a slow death.

By April 2006, however, Brown was backing down. He retreated from previous estimates that the whole enterprise was unaffordable and would cost the exchequer £8 billion, instead accepting '90 per cent to 95 per cent' of the report. The compromise required was that the link between the state pension and earnings, along with many of the other reforms, would not start in 2010 but be delayed until 2012.

It might have taken nearly ten years, but at last it looked as though Labour was prepared to engage with one of the biggest social policy issues that faces any country. After endless fudges, rearguard actions and some astonishingly bad decision-making, there was at last a coherent plan. Even so, Britain had fallen way behind other Western governments, including Sweden, Australia and New Zealand, which over the past decade have started to build up far more secure superannuation arrangements.

The Pensions Commission, which had had such an inauspicious start, managed in the end to see most of its proposals turned into legislation. This was no mean achievement given the squabbling between Number 10 and the Treasury and New Labour's appalling record of pension reform. Having navigated these rapids Turner found himself shuffled into the role of chairman of the Financial Services Authority in 2008 – in the midst of the credit crunch – possibly the least desirable job in government given its failings over a number of years, from the Equitable Life debacle to the banking meltdown in 2007–8. Paradoxically, if the FSA survives in anything like its present form

Turner could find himself having to deal with some of its regulatory shortfalls should his pensions reform turn rancid.

And then pension reform hit the brick wall of the credit crisis. In his Pre-Budget Report of December 2009 Chancellor Alastair Darling laid out Britain's perilous fiscal situation. The budget deficit was forecast to hit £180 billion in the tax year ending in April 2010. Even with proposed public spending cuts and tax increases the national debt would reach 78 per cent of national output by 2014–15. In the battle to defeat the national budgetary crisis pension provision would once again find itself in the front line. Tax relief on pensions for people earning more than £150,000 would be severely curtailed. Darling also disclosed that the Personal Account, one of the core Turner reforms, was being delayed. A footnote to the Pre-Budget Report – that Turner's auto-enrolment scheme for those without pensions would be delayed, saving the government £0.7 billion in 2013–14 and £1.6 billion in 2014–15. It was a massive blow to the prospects of the scheme getting off the ground in spite of more than five years of infighting, debate and planning.

Despite the budgetary crisis Brown's government behaved as if nothing had changed. On 12 January 2010 the pensions minister Angela Eagle announced that the Personal Account would be renamed the National Employment Savings Trust (NEST) after a rebranding exercise which had cost the taxpayer £363,000. She declared:

This government's radical reforms to the pensions system will ensure millions of workers on low and moderate incomes are able to save for retirement in a workplace pension with a guaranteed minimum contribution from their employer. NEST will play a key role in this and help transform attitudes to saving.

But behind the grandiose words the reality was very different. The Pre-Budget-Report undid much of the good work of the previous five years, with the future of the Personal Account/NEST thrown into confusion. Similarly, the closely linked promise to restore the earnings link for state pensions in 2012 was also in doubt.

Labour's big pension reform had been held up at the budget warning light and it was not clear that the next government, whatever its colour, would fully back the hard-won retirement revolution.

CHAPTER 10

The Labour legacy

A health check on pensions after 13 years of Labour in office does not make for particularly cheery reading: private and company pensions in retreat, the state pension facing an uncertain future, public-sector pensions out of control, the strategic path ahead far from clear.

On the surface, the government decision to adopt the Turner Report recommendation about the state pension should have given its recipients some cause for celebration. Promising to link adjustments to the pension to salary rather than price increases ensured that many would face a brighter future. The miserliness of the state pension, among the worst in Western Europe, was a national disgrace. Linking it to earnings would have helped bring it up to scratch. It would also have allowed millions of elderly people to escape from the complexities and stigma associated with means testing.

The trade-off – a planned increase in the state retirement age – looked to be a fair quid pro quo. It was also recognition of the fact that, with private pensions in retreat, the state needed to do more to bolster the nation's retirement prospects.

The first hints of a delay in the return of earnings-adjusted state pensions came in Alistair Darling's December 2009 Pre-Budget Report. At the same time the dire state of public finances also made it inevitable that, whatever happened to the pension itself, the state retirement age would still have to rise. People were left with the worst of both worlds. The promise of an earnings-related state pension remained, but the ominous words 'subject to affordability and the fiscal position' meant that no one could be quite sure when that promise might be fulfilled.

Uncertainty also surrounded the main Turner proposal taken up by the government: the creation of a National Pensions Savings Scheme (NPSS). Initially referred to as BritSave, it was officially called the Personal Account before this was replaced by another acronym NEST in early 2010. The essential feature of this new semi-private plan was that it would be compulsory for employers – every firm big or small would have to offer a form of occupational pension to its workforce – and all employees would be enrolled automatically.

Only those members of staff who specifically asked to opt out would be allowed to do so. The goal was to bring into the occupational net the 56 per cent of the population which Turner estimated had no retirement provision at all. It would aim to be low-cost – the initial goal of the delivery authority being to keep the price of running the system below 0.5 per cent – and to offer a choice of savings vehicles to joiners.

Staff would pay in 4 per cent of their salaries and employers 3 per cent with an extra 1 per cent coming from the government in tax relief. Employer contributions were to be phased in over three years. Broadly, this contribution would be at a reduced 1 per cent for the first year after the requirement came into force, then 2 per cent for the second year, then the full amount in the third. If the maths worked, not a given in the light of past government savings accounting, a typical earner ought to receive a retirement income equivalent to 45 per cent of earnings. One-third would come from NEST (otherwise known as the Personal Account) – or an occupational scheme – and the rest through the enhanced earnings-linked state pension. With a total 8 per cent of salary going into the scheme, somebody earning £25,000 a year could end up with a NEST pension of £167 a month. Employers and individuals would be able put in more if they wished. Workers could also keep their accounts when they moved jobs.

NEST pensions were to be set up by the delivery authority and then run by an independent board similar to a set of pension fund trustees. It was estimated that if the scheme was delivered on time, by 2040 it would have £200 billion of assets under investment. The scheme was designed to be an independent workplace pension that could be used by any employer and would make saving for retirement the norm for up to ten million workers on low to middle incomes – those aged 22–65 earning from just over £5,000 up to £33,500 a year. Pensions Secretary John Hutton – who had the initial job of selling the plan to a sceptical Parliament and public – argued it was to overcome the 'inertia and short-termism' that was stopping people making financial decisions, particularly in low-income households. Hutton saw NEST as part of a package of measures including the restoration of the earnings link and reduced means testing.

For those buying into the scheme a limited range of choices would be on offer. These might include a social and ethical fund for the socially conscious investor; a sharia fund to cater for Britain's growing number of Muslims; a 'guaranteed' fund for those who would prefer most of their money to be held in cash and bonds together – pre-existing 'pool funds' run by experienced private-sector fund managers. The money would be held at arm's length from government, in the hands of small teams of professional trustees.

Obviously, it was recognised that the success or otherwise of the plans would depend in part on how the funds, which would build up very quickly into billions of pounds, were invested. Instead of a great suite of private-sector choices, as is the case in Sweden (and to a lesser extent in Britain's system of child trust fund saving), the assumption was that most of the money – perhaps as much as 80 per cent – would be earmarked for a 'safe' default fund with minimum risk. This was because the bulk of those initially involved would be economically unsophisticated and not want to make an investment choice.

The plan was certainly not without its critics. Tony Blair, fearful of a backlash from business, was not entirely comfortable. Predictably, the CBI disliked the additional burden placed on business, viewing it as another typical New Labour stealth tax. Then there was the issue of implementation. A vast new computer system would be required, far more complex that those used to administer similar schemes in countries such as Sweden. In the wake of the NHS systems debacle, that alone gave some pause for thought.

Even John Hutton expressed some unease, telling me in late 2009, after he had resigned from Gordon Brown's government:

> All of this looked basically affordable and we thought it would work. I still think it would work. It would lose the fog about means testing and makes the state pension as a result more valuable. But I think you can never tell. What will they say of Turner in 20 years from now, that is the crucial test. We all felt at the time that this was a very, very significant reform that had the potential to deal with one of Britain's fundamental failures, which was to make proper provision for people in old age. If personal accounts don't succeed we will be back to square one.

There were also some major strategic issues. Research done by the respected think tank the Institute of Fiscal Studies suggested that for a far larger number of people than that estimated by Turner and the Department of Work and Pensions saving through NEST would be a hardship. They simply wouldn't have enough money to put aside. What's more, it would make no economic sense for them. Their incomes were so low that they would always be candidates for means-tested benefits rather than a personal account. In other words NEST would have exactly the same shortcomings as Ron Sandler's stakeholder pension.

Turner told me that he was aware of this danger and it was one of the reasons he wishes he had been more revolutionary by proposing aggressive increases in the state pension and the elimination of means testing. Consultant Ros Altmann has voiced her fears that the personal account aspect of the scheme might in time lead to another huge mis-selling scandal. Were the pension delivered to be less than that promised, or if the worker could have done just as well without saving at all and claiming government benefits, the whole system could be challenged.

The biggest concern expressed by critics, though, and one already manifesting itself – with the Aon decision to cut back its contributions the most obvious example – is that instead of building pension saving the scheme would kill occupational plans as we know them stone dead. The availability of a cheaper alternative meant that employers would have a ready-made way of reducing pension costs and liabilities. Instead of paying anything from 7 per cent to 15 or more per cent into current defined salary and contribution plans, firms would be able to cut the cost of funding pensions dramatically by trading down to the minimum of 3 per cent required by government. NEST has the potential to finish the job that Gordon Brown began with his initial tax raid on pension funds. By so doing it would condemn a large part of the population, currently saving in the expectation of a reasonably comfortable pension, to something akin to retirement poverty.

Turner was adamant that even if this happened it was a price worth paying. 'You had to decide the most important social priority,' he told me in the summer of 2009. 'There is a danger that if you do set a national standard that people will come down to that level. On the other hand, if you don't set it, you will have a whole lot of people who have no private provision at all. That proportion is now 56 per cent and has gone up from 44 per cent over the last 10 to 15 years.' He sardonically suggested that such opposition seen in the newspapers stemmed from the fact that editors and reporters are among the haves rather than the have-nots.

The proposed timing of Britain's launch of the new venture could not have been worse. It came after the economic boom descended into bust, when confidence in government and financial institutions was at a low ebb and family budgets stretched to the limit by inflation. And then a whole new element of doubt was added when Alistair Darling slowed down implementation in late 2009. Altmann for one was delighted, hoping this might lead to the scheme being cancelled altogether. In a press release headed 'Empty NESTs and cracked eggs' she declared, 'The project should be put on hold. It is dangerous and will contribute further to the destruction of our once thriving pensions saving culture.' Frank Field, who saw the need for reform way back in 2007, was similarly harsh. 'The message has gone out that the government will help those who can't save or won't save,' he wrote. 'Woe betide those who do save. They will be mocked. Forty per cent of the population cannot now make themselves better off by saving than they can by simply spending now and relying on the state later. A free society cannot, in the long run, survive on this basis.'

The uncertainty about the future of NEST serves to throw the spotlight back on the terrible fate of private pensions under New Labour over the previous 13 years. When Lord Turner issued his report in 2005, 60,000 occupational schemes were being wound up. Five sixths of the final salary schemes that had closed their doors by 2010 did so on Labour's watch. Even companies with robust and well-funded schemes, such as Europe's biggest oil company BP, closed their final salary schemes to new members.

In trying to deal with a fast-deteriorating situation, the government first applied a series of bandages before attempting to find a cure for the condition. Compensation had been around for a couple of years when Labour came to power: the 1995 Pensions Act, set up in the wake of the Maxwell scandal, offered protection to members of company pension schemes suffering actual or potential loss of pension through theft or other dishonesty. In seeking to compensate those who had already suffered, Labour put its faith in the Financial Assistance Scheme (FAS) and its more professional successor the Pension Protection Fund (PPF). This was a belt-and-braces response to the growing problem of protecting the rights of members of retirement schemes in insolvent companies. If criminal activity had been the previous driving force for compensation, incompetence or plain poor performance now largely shaped Labour's guarantees to pensioners and future retirees in companies whose funds had gone under.

The FAS was set up to assist individuals suffering hardship who had lost pension rights because they were members of underfunded pension schemes. It was responsible for sorting out the interests of fund members whose schemes went into wind-up between January 1997 and April 2005. It also covered employees in firms that became insolvent before March 2006. Compensation was to be paid in the form of a top-up to provide the member with 90 per cent of the pension they were expecting to receive with a cap of £26,000 a year. But it had required a sustained media and parliamentary campaign – including flamboyant demonstrations at Labour Party conferences – to drag this deal out of the Treasury. Moreover, the scheme was hampered by footling bureaucracy that at times looked to obstruct rather than help victims of collapse.

To cope with the growing number of pension funds going into wind-up and limit its own exposure, the government then launched the Pension Protection Fund in 2006. This was essentially an insurance scheme funded by the rest of the industry which offered compensation equal to 90 per cent of expected benefits to future pensioners caught up in insolvency and 100 per cent to those already in receipt of pensions. The PPF was a direct response to the wind-up scandal – to which Labour had been so slow to respond – but paradoxically did not cover those who had actually campaigned for compensation. (The reason for this was that the PPF was paid for by a levy on healthy pension schemes, and to have made it pay for past mistakes might have looked like a form of retrospective taxation and might have undermined industry support.) Earlier victims, therefore, were left to the tender mercies of the FAS. The government estimated that from 1998 some 65,000 people had lost 20 per cent or more of their anticipated occupational pensions when their employers went bust. With more than 125 final salary pension schemes being wound up in 2003–4 alone, the government believed the PPF would end the 'tragedy' of workers being left empty-handed.

Critics of the scheme soon spotted its flaws. Payments into the PPF would discourage those firms still running final salary pension funds from keeping them in place. It also was feared that the PPF might not have sufficient funds to cope if a company with a huge pensions deficit collapsed. 'Businesses at most risk and most likely to call on the PPF should pay more,' argued former CBI Director General Sir Digby Jones. 'The fund could be in trouble if a proper risk-based approach is not swiftly implemented. Businesses must not face an ever-increasing cost burden.' The omens were not good. The American equivalent, which had been around for much longer, had a black hole of tens of billions of dollars.

The credit crunch of 2007, followed by the banking collapse and global recession, made things a lot worse. UK final salary schemes fell even deeper into the red and in the autumn of 2008 it was estimated that nearly 8,000 private sector schemes were collectively in deficit to the tune of £97.3 billion.

All this put increasing pressure on the PPF, which was on the alert for an influx of firms whose schemes needed bailing out. The 2009 collapse of the Canadian telecoms giant Nortel triggered one of Britain's biggest pension fund blow-ups. Nortel's pension scheme, which had more than 43,000 members, was placed in the PPF with an estimated deficit of £1 billion. Nortel's collapse swelled the PPF's responsibilities, which in its first four years of operation had amassed billions of pounds of liabilities. Ironically, the chief executive of the PPF, Alan Rubinstein, an urbane banker, had been recruited from the bankrupt broker-dealer Lehman Brothers, which would also become a client of the PPF.

Rubinstein was determined not to place too much pressure on the rest of the pensions system and fought to hold the levy at £700 million for three years. Speaking in June 2009 he warned, however, that once the financial crisis and recession of 2007–9 had passed 'we will consider in the future raising the amount of the levy we collect above the rate of inflation'. He shared the worry that some monster final salary pension scheme might end up in the PPF, seriously undermining the funding of the insurance fund. In particular he was working closely with the chairman of the Pensions Regulator David Norgrove to monitor the health of the biggest deficit funds including British Telecom, with a massive £9 billion deficit, and British Airways, with a £4 billion shortfall.

As for the future, there will be no more attractive target for finance directors looking for instant wins than the company contributions paid into pension funds. This is especially true at a time when companies are forced to reveal pension deficits on an annual basis in their report and accounts, as well as undertake regular more-comprehensive actuarial valuations. All the pressure from David Norgrove is to give priority to pensions funding and for companies to disclose plans to close the deficit over time. Indeed, putting money aside for pension deficits is seen as important as rewarding investors with dividends. An easy way out of this conflict may well be to slash pension costs and benefits. The future of pensions in the private sector is grim indeed.

By contrast, things seem rather more rosy for the five million people working in the UK public sector. The 'gold-plated' public-sector pensions system has been largely immune to the forces that have brought occupational and personal plans to their knees. The standard defence for public-sector pensions is that public servants have traditionally earned less than their counterparts in the private sector and therefore deserve some degree of compensation in their overall package. Lord Turner, for example, believes it is 'valuable for the public sector to be saying quite a significant chunk of total remuneration is in pension rights. We have lower salaries for the equivalent job but we have higher pensions. I think that is a useful contribution across the whole pension market.' He also – rather bizarrely – has suggested that public-sector pensions 'set a benchmark to which the bigger firms in the private sector then need to respond'.

The basic argument seems fair enough. The problem is that it now appears to be based on a false proposition. Quite simply, state employment has become as financially rewarding as working in the corporate sector, except for those at the very top. And even there remuneration is pretty generous. Executives at government-owned enterprises such as the Royal Mail and Network Rail are in receipt of pay deals every bit as generous as those in some FTSE 100 board-rooms. Local authority chieftains now earn salaries that more than compare with their counterparts in industry. Post-credit-crunch official data shows that gross annual pay in the public sector is now higher than that in the private sector for all but the top 25 per cent. Hourly pay is higher for all but the top 10 per cent, and the public sector enjoys more job security and longer holidays than most people in the wealth-creating part of the economy. The Pensions Policy Institute, an independent research charity, estimated average public-sector salaries at £25,600 and those in the private sector at £25,300.

Yet in Britain's febrile political universe the uniquely protected nature of public-sector pensions is an issue which dare not speak its name. When the Conservative leader David Cameron briefly referred to the issue in an informal address in Manchester in 2008 it was quickly expunged from the public record. New Labour was presented with the chance to impose reforms in 2005 but baulked at the opportunity, even though this threatened to undermine efforts by Turner to modernise Britain's crumbling retirement edifice. If any politician from the mainstream parties is considering reform they are keeping their intentions well disguised. The drive for change has come largely from employers' groups like the CBI and the Institute of Directors (IoD) and think tanks such as the Institute of Economic Affairs (IEA). Critics like the free-market IoD have gone as far as to refer to the mismatch as a 'pension apartheid' between those working for government and those in the entrepreneurial sector of the economy.

The situation, then, is that as pensions in the private sector go to the wall, those in the public sector are very nicely looked after. Most public-sector schemes still operate a pension age of 60. Indeed, critical staff such as police officers are allowed to quit work in their mid-50s with a full pension and may then choose to embark on a new career. Retired police officers, for example, may opt to boost their enhanced public pensions by almost immediately taking on work in the private security industry.

Public-sector pensions are also not just salary-linked but also index-linked, which means they keep pace with inflation. Some public-sector workers enjoy a privilege known as the 'rule of 85'. This allows those whose age and years of service add up to 85 to claim full pension for the years they have put in, an arrangement which no private-sector employer could match. What's more, many public-sector pensions are non-contributory, a claim sometimes disputed by members of public-sector plans, who insist that they make a notional contribution through their department.

As the size of the public sector has ballooned under New Labour by up to one million workers (excluding those in the semi-nationalised banks), so the number of active members of these final salary schemes has soared. It increased from 4.2 million in 1995 to 5.2 million in 2007. Among those are: 1.3 million health workers, 1.6 million in local government, 600,000 teachers, 600,000 civil servants, 200,000 in the armed forces, 150,000 police officers and 50,000 firemen. Compared with these figures, final salary schemes are enjoyed by just 16 per cent of those working in private-sector companies.

Employee contributions went up in 2008, with teachers paying 6.4 per cent of salary (up from 6 per cent), and NHS workers between 5 per cent and 8.5 per cent (also up from 6 per cent). But the police saw their contributions cut from 11 per cent to 9.5 per cent of salary, and firemen from 11 per cent to 8.5 per cent. Members of the armed forces make no contribution and their pay is lower as a result. Contributions made by local authority workers, who were paying 6 per cent, are now on a sliding scale between 5.5 per cent and

7.5 per cent. The cost to the taxpayer of a pension for a teacher or policeman on modest earnings can come to anything between £350,000 and £500,000. Estimates suggest that some GPs have pension pots well in excess of £1 million.

Simultaneously, unfunded public-sector pension liabilities have soared. The official estimate of the deficit by the Office of National Statistics in January 2010 stood at £770 billion, or 59 per cent of national output. The employers' organisation the CBI calculates the public-sector shortfall at £915 billion, or 64 per cent of GDP. At the very top end is the figure of £1 trillion projected by the free market think tank the Institute of Economic Affairs (IEA). Even if the more modest numbers are accepted, the figures remain alarming. The government isn't very helpful here because it buries away its liabilities in the complexity of consolidated fund accounting. Whereas firms are obliged to publish an annual assessment of the state of their pension funds – under Financial Reporting Standard 17 (FRS17) – there is no such obligation in Whitehall.

It is scarcely surprising that campaigns should have been mounted to bring the retirement age for public-sector workers into line with the national retirement age. Nor is it altogether surprising that some have pushed for workers in the state sector to be enrolled in the new 'personal account' or NEST when it starts to operate from 2012 (assuming it does) on the grounds that at least then there will be some incentive to make the scheme work and that some cap might be put on the future liability for paying public-sector pensions.

But politicians have so far ducked the issue. Tony Blair and Alan Johnson blinked in 2005, and no one has really tried since. Labour has not wanted to run the risk of a public fight with the unions. Many state jobs are located in Labour heartlands such as the North-West and North-East of England, and in Scotland, and messing with benefits could have electoral repercussions.

Meanwhile pension pots among the great and the good have continued to grow. Of course the average chief executive among the top FTSE 100 companies does pretty nicely too. The rewards he or she receives have at times looked grotesque and have over recent years been bid up by pay committees on the grounds of international competition and the like. In many cases the hurdles for achieving bonuses and the ease with which vast pension pots have been built up – most notoriously in the case of Royal Bank of Scotland banker Sir Fred Goodwin – have been outrageous. Goodwin left with a pension pot valued at £16.6 million, although this was eventually cut back in the face of public anger.

Public servants won't ever get to this sort of level. On the other hand, unlike the Goodwins of this world they do have far greater job security, and the pensions that they are now achieving at age 60 have, by any reasonable standard, become extraordinarily large. In November 2007, for instance, Sir Richard Mottram became the country's wealthiest state pensioner when he retired from the Cabinet Office on a package worth almost £2.7 million. This allowed him to withdraw a tax-free lump sum of £335,000 and an annual pension of £110,000.

When in December 2008 the pension prospects of permanent secretaries, the senior civil servants in their departments, were released, the scale of the pensions built up was eye-popping. Leigh Lewis, at the Department for Work and Pensions – whose department has presided over Britain's pension meltdown – had accumulated a pot worth £1,881,000. At the Home Office Sir David Normington's fund had reached £1,785,000.

Outside the corridors of Whitehall Sir Ian Blair, removed as the Metropolitan Police Commissioner early in 2009, could look forward to a reported £5 million pension pot. In the shires Peter Gould, 54, quit his £215,000-a-year post as chief executive of Northamptonshire County Council in February 2007. He was set to receive a lump sum of £291,000 and a guaranteed annual pension of £97,000 after just seven years of service. And over at the licence-fee-funded BBC, Jenny Abramsky, its veteran director of audio, had built up a pension pot of £4 million by the time she stepped down in the autumn of 2008. This provided her with an annual pension of £190,000 – a clearly astonishing amount of money for anyone on the public payroll. John Smith, head of Worldwide, the BBC's commercial arm, has a £3.1 million pot, arts guru Alan Yentob £2.8 million and the Deputy Director General Mark Byford £2.7 million.

Ginger group the Taxpayers' Alliance, using data obtained through the Freedom of Information Act to reveal the full extent of the generosity of public-sector pension arrangements, found in 2009 that some 3,680 retired public-sector employees were in receipt of an annual pension (not including any lump sum) of at least £33,000. This implied total retirement benefits each of at least £1 million. Overall, the Institute for Economic Affairs estimated in 2006 public-sector pension liabilities at more than £40,000 for every household in the country.

In June 2009 the *Sunday Times* compiled a new rich list of public-sector pension millionaires, which showed that there were no fewer than 22,999 seven-figure pension pots. You can bet they were not nurses, orderlies, ambulance drivers and staff in the front line. Amazingly, the list included 3,680 former civil servants and 2,658 teachers, along with some 400 retired staff from Glasgow City Council and 223 from Kent County Council.

Top of the public-sector pension league was Bank of England Governor Mervyn King, who by June 2009 had accumulated a pension pot of £5.4 million. Chief of the Defence Staff Sir Jock Stirrup had accumulated a pension of £2.4 million. Also in the top ten was the man closest to power, Cabinet Secretary Sir Gus O'Donnell, with £2 million. At the time of Labour's private-sector pension raid in 1997 the laconic and politically savvy O'Donnell was a Treasury mandarin.

Such largesse in the public sector may just be the tip of an iceberg. Corin Taylor of the Taxpayers' Alliance warned in June 2009 that the number of million-pound public-sector pension pots is set to increase dramatically in the short to medium term, with 123,000 civil servants above the age of 50 working in 2007, compared with 88,000 in 1996. The Cabinet Office, possibly fearful of charges of greed, countered by stressing that all new entrants to the Civil Service had a pension based on career earnings rather than their final salary and that there were penalties for taking it before 65. Maybe, but those already inside the system, the very people who have been dictating Britain's pensions rules for decades, still have final salary schemes and the right to leave at 60 because of government cowardice in tackling the issue in 2005.

Public rewards at their most extreme became apparent during the MPs' expenses scandal of 2009. Daily public exposure of Members of Parliament of all parties openly abusing, and in some cases cheating on allowances, caused a public outcry rarely seen in modern times. It was barely possible for a senior minister or MP to appear on the BBC's *Question Time* stage without being booed by audiences made up of a cross-section of the British public.

The nation's reputation for reasonably civilised political discourse took a nasty blow. It was 'ordeal by *Daily Telegraph*', as the traditionally Tory newspaper used its acquisition of a Commons database to reveal who had been claiming for what and how much. Among the more outrageous items on the MPs' roll of dishonour were 'phantom' mortgages and dodging Capital Gains Tax. Expenses claims veered from the sublime to the ridiculous, from purchases of dog food and bars of chocolates to paying for 'duck houses' and cleaning the moat of a grand country home. It provided an all-too-unsavoury glimpse of abuse of power by the very people who impose laws and rules on the lives of ordinary people.

The expenses scandal also refocused attention on the issue of MPs' salaries and pensions. But Parliament sought to keep the facts as far removed from the eyes of the voters as is possible in a democratic system. When I first ventured to write about MPs' generous pension arrangements in the *Daily Mail* in 2000, the ire of several members of what we now know to have been a rampaging rogue institution fell upon me.

Now we have a clearer idea of what has been going on it's pretty clear that MPs will not face old age on a state pension of £97.65 a week, bumped up to £132.60 with the means-tested Pension Credit. Rather, after 26 years of service, they can look forward to a guaranteed index-linked pension of £38,000 a year, much of it transferable to their widow or widower after death. The dozen or so MPs most embroiled in the expenses scandal – with behaviour verging in criminality – will receive a taxpayer-subsidised retirement fund worth on average more than £1 million each. It is possible perhaps to justify most MPs' exceptional arrangements on the grounds that many hold office for short periods and so do not have job security and are in a perilous position. A cynic working in the private sector, though, might respond that he or she is in the same position.

The largesse of MPs' pensions arises from a scheme that dates from 2001, when the Commons voted for their entitlement to accrue at an annual rate of 50 per cent faster than most of the public sector. Each pension pot is based on available annuity rates, length of service and the age of the MP. Moreover, although MPs pay around 10 per cent of their salary into a pension plan – an element of which is based on length of service – they are not covering anything like the full costs and they enjoy considerable protection. An MP will not suffer, for example, if the actuaries calculating the cost of his or her pension scheme get their sums wrong; the taxpayers will pick up the tab. In July 2009 the final vote in the Commons – as MPs headed off to their constituencies for an 80-day summer break – was to correct a shortfall in their pension fund. Moreover, MPs, like many others in the public sector, have not been affected by the dividend tax changes which devastated occupational pensions in the late 1990s.

Ministers enjoy even greater pension provision. By 2009 Gordon Brown's pot for being in the top job was worth £274,000, which adds £19,000 a year to his MP's retirement pay. Having been an MP longer, Justice Secretary Jack Straw would get £294,000 – paying out an annual pension of £20,520 – while Chancellor Alistair Darling's was worth £235,000, paying out £16,400. As Tom McPhail, head of pension research at respected investment advisers Hargreaves Landsdown, commented, 'The MPs' pension scheme is overdue for fundamental reform. It allows an MP to retire on the equivalent of the national average wage after only around 17 years' work. How can this be justified?'

Technically, the Senior Salaries Review Body (SSRB) is responsible for setting MPs' pay, allowances and pensions in line with those of the Civil Service. However, the Commons has the final say on any recommendations, and down the years MPs have voted in the Commons at regular intervals for their own pension arrangements. The current scheme – the Parliamentary Contributory Pension Fund – came into being four years after New Labour took office. When MPs planned their first increase, the late Robin Cook, then leader of the House, warned them to consider whether they should accept 'an even wider gap' between their pensions and those of people working in hospitals, schools and local government.

By July 2002 members had decided not to heed Cook's advice and were agreeing an enhanced deal which had two key elements. Contributions would increase from 6 per cent to 9 per cent (they later rose further). More significantly, MPs would not have to serve as long to receive the full pension. Chairman of the MPs' pension trustees Sir John Butterfill said the rise was justified, and it was voted through by a committee of 20 members. The *Daily Mail* revealed at the time that these measures were opposed by the SSRB, which wanted MPs to accrue their pensions at the existing rate. Not all MPs liked the idea either. Attacking the proposals, Steve Webb, the Liberal Democrat pensions spokesman, voiced the thoughts of many when he said, 'We look as though we are completely out of touch.'

Year by year the sums involved have been mounting, but nobody can be sure of the true cost to the taxpayer. The SSRB estimated it at

22 per cent of salary in 2008, compared with teachers at 13 per cent. John Ralfe, an independent pension consultant who made his reputation as the shrewd manager of the Boots the Chemist scheme, reckoned the real cost for MPs was more like 48 per cent of pay.

The annual report of the House of Commons in 2008, meanwhile, was showing that MPs' pensions could end up costing the public purse more than twice the sum originally thought. Official estimates showed that the Treasury would be paying £7.8 million every year for MPs' pensions – equivalent to 18.1 per cent of their salaries. However, a footnote in the accounts admitted that this figure could be as high as £16.5 million a year – 38 per cent of salaries.

Pension campaigners have accused MPs of setting themselves up at the head of a public-sector 'pensions aristocracy'. Ros Altmann observed in a 2009 paper that MPs had consistently voted themselves 'something more than generous'. This did not go unnoticed by newer members of the political class. By the end of 2008 Members of the Scottish Parliament were casting covetous eyes on the pensions of MPs at Westminster and seeking a similar package. They sought to join the gravy train by increasing their own pension rights.

Early in 2009 it emerged in a Commons reply that the cost of MPs' pensions had risen by 25 per cent over five years, from £9.8 million in 2003 to £12 million in 2008. A further £15 million had been put in to plug a £100 million black hole caused by a contributions holiday from the scheme between 1989 and 2003. Paul Rowen, who succeeded Webb as Liberal Democrat pensions spokesman, said, 'This extravagance is an insult to hard-pressed taxpayers and should be reviewed. MPs need to tighten their belts too.' Tom McPhail at Hargreaves Landsdown remarked, 'The scheme is unsustainably generous. It exists in a different world to the 28 million working taxpayers.'

Before the expenses scandal blew up Gordon Brown, sensing growing public disapproval, recognised the tide of opinion was turning against the benefits culture for the ruling elite. In January 2008 he volunteered to forgo his grace-and-favour PM's pension, which he could draw when he leaves office, until he was 65. Giving up this entitlement could cost him £450,000 if he were to retire from Parliament early. In February 2009 he wrote to the Senior Salaries Review Body suggesting a series of reforms to the MPs' scheme including increasing the pension age, changing provisions for retirement, lowering the maximum level of benefits and, most significantly, moving away from a final salary scheme to a less-generous defined contribution structure. He asked the SSRB chairman to consider the 'full range of options' for reducing the £12 million annual burden. Increasing the retirement age or ending the current final salary scheme was included.

In July 2009, as the expenses scandal blew up, Brown took further action. A scheme had been drafted under which an extra £800,000 a year of taxpayers' cash would go into the fund, which faced a £51 million deficit. As part of the deal MPs were to be asked to find an extra £60 a month from their salaries. Brown, however, abandoned the plan to make the taxpayers fund a large part of the MPs' pension scheme shortfall.

Clearly, when it comes to public-sector pensions, something needs to give. Sustaining a system in which, almost uniquely, nearly all of the country's public-sector workers can look forward to an index-linked pension based on the salary that they are earning at the point when they retire has become the economics of the madhouse. Such pensions have survived not because they have been better managed than private-sector pensions but because they are subsidised by taxpayers.

Reforms to date have been modest. The Turner Commission declined to consider the option of using some of the money spent on public-sector pensioners to provide a better state pension for all. Alan Johnson's deal in 2005 did increase the retirement age for teachers, NHS workers and civil servants from 60 to 65, but only for new recruits. It also stipulated that new civil servants be paid a pension based on their average salary at retirement, not their final salary, but the government's own figures estimate that these changes will only save about £13 billion over the next 50 years.

Indeed, the new arrangements for some of the schemes actually managed to push up rather than cut the bill. Under the old scheme, for example, teachers received a pension of half their final salary plus a lump sum of three years' pension, if they worked for 40 years. So, if someone retired on an average teacher's salary, they might receive a pension of around £16,000 a year and a lump sum of around £40,000. The new arrangements offer no lump sum, but they do provide a better pension. The same teacher retiring today might receive a pension of £21,300 a year.

Police officers were able to retire on two-thirds of their pension after 30 years, so if they were earning a typical £34,000 they might retire on a pension of more than £22,000. This has now changed for new recruits, who will have to work for 35 years to get a full pension. They will then receive only half their final salary, but will get a lump sum of four times the pension.

Despite these changes, the cost to the public purse has soared. In 2009 it emerged that taxpayers would have to find an extra £2.3 billion a year to fund public sector pensions, as a black hole in the Government's finances was set to double in four years. The small print figures at the back of the Red Book, which details Budget measures, showed that the shortfall covered by the Treasury in 2007–8 was £2.3 billion; forecasts show that by 2011 this will have grown to £4.6 billion.

Pressure for change, however, has been growing. Paul Rowen, MP for Rochdale and Liberal Democrat pensions spokesman, called on MPs in early 2009 to seize the initiative and change their pension arrangements as a first step to wider public-sector pension reform. He added, 'Urgent reform is needed. We have suggested a pension commission similar to the New Zealand Retirement Commission. This would look at all aspects of public-sector pensions, including funding and benefits.'

Previously, in January 2008, Conservative leader David Cameron had made his short-lived contribution to the debate by proposing the closure of the 'very generous' public-sector final salary scheme to new entrants. He said that allowing the scheme to continue endlessly was 'not appropriate' and called for a switch to defined contributions in a bid to bridge the growing pensions gap with most of the rest of society. He told business leaders in Manchester:

> We are getting into a situation now where pretty much everyone in the private sector has gone to defined contributions and the final salary schemes are closed. My vision over time is to move increasingly towards defined contribution rather than final salary schemes. There is an issue of fairness between the private sector and the public sector but there is also an issue of economic efficiency. This is something where the government has been remarkably feeble, partly because they are in hock to the public-sector unions.

The CBI has been at the forefront of the campaign for a re-examination of public-sector pensions. It has called for an independent commission, a review of retirement ages and urged the government to come clean about the ballooning cost of public sector pensions. It calculated in December 2008 that unfunded government schemes had liabilities of over £915 billion. The Institute of Directors has called for a reduction in the cost to taxpayers of unfunded public-sector pensions. It added, 'The current recession will make the pensions apartheid even greater and the enormous deficits being run intensify the need to reduce long-term costs to help bring the public finances back to stability. There really is no alternative.'

The media too has voiced concerns. Commentator Dominic Lawson, writing in the *Sunday Times* in February 2009, for example, described the government's obligations to meet the cost of public-sector pensions as a 'giant Ponzi scheme':

By contrast [to the private sector] the index-linked final salary obligations of the public sector are legally enforceable – no matter what happens to the British economy, there is no way a future government can adjust the amounts to be paid in future to current (and retired) state employees . . . In the last resort, a government knows that it does not have to find the money to meet its obligations: it can just print the stuff.

It's only in recent years that some acceptance of this at the top of government has started to become apparent. In part this has been a result of the coming of the credit crunch in 2007, the subsequent global banking crisis in the autumn of 2008, and then the steepest recession since the 1930s. As the torrent of tax income from the City of London, which had produced a dividend of £200 billion for the exchequer in the decade to 2007, started to dry up, Britain's public finances began to look very sick indeed. With the Treasury having to support the banking system and the mortgage market to the tune of up to £1 trillion, the need to look for cost savings elsewhere became ever more urgent.

Ahead of his May 2009 Budget Alistair Darling signalled he might slash public-sector pensions to squeeze state spending. With an election only 12 months away, in something of a deathbed conversion he told the IoD that reforms were being lined up. Current teachers, nurses and police would hold on to their deals, but future employees were being targeted for cuts. 'There has to be equity whether people are employed in the public or private sector,' he said. 'It comes down to a sense of fairness. You have got to be fair to existing scheme members . . . but, looking ahead over the next few years, we have to make sure we live within our means.' For their part, senior Tories said that in the event of a Conservative victory at the polls in 2010 the whole issue would be referred to the Office of Budget Responsibility, a new independent fiscal arm of government.

The case for picking up the pace was reinforced when the true cost of pensions for all current public-sector workers was estimated at £1.2 trillion in a June 2009 report from the British-North American Committee. This was the equivalent of £20,000 for every man, woman and child in Britain. The committee, made up of academics and business leaders, argued that the Treasury was greatly understating the cost of providing gold-plated retirement schemes for public-sector workers.

Nobody wants to see public-sector pensions reduced. There are many tales of hardship at the lower end of the pay scales, and, of course, most public workers make a terrific contribution to society as a whole. But, thanks to what has happened to the private sector, everything is now out of kilter. It is this which has given rise to the pension apartheid accusation. As government jobs and pensions proliferated during New Labour's time in office the steady flow of companies closing their final salary schemes developed into a torrent.

The pension situation in Britain is grim. For 56 per cent of the population there is no provision at all other than a rotten state pension supported by humiliating and complex means testing. Those in the public sector have a pension system that is now unsustainable and can no longer be defended. Those in the private sector have seen their pensions plundered, undermined and in many cases destroyed altogether.

New Labour has devastated a pensions legacy which just a decade ago seemed so strong. The influential Paris-based Organisation for Economic Cooperation and Development placed Britain at the bottom of an international pension league table for those yet to retire in a report issued in June 2009. In the same month research by the Office for National Statistics confirmed just how little the state pension is worth. In response the charity Age Concern commented, 'It is a national disgrace that more than two million pensioners are trapped in poverty.'

There is now a mountain to climb and massive liabilities for future governments to deal with. The public-sector pensions shortfall grows ever larger, there is a gaping hole in the commitments of the Pension Protection Fund and the universal state pension remains as mean as ever.

It's not a legacy that New Labour should be proud of.

CHAPTER 11

The shape of things to come?

In March 2007 the wealthy Italian deputy chairman of Alliance Boots, Stefano Pessina, launched an audacious bid for the chemists group with the help of New York-based private equity kings Kohlberg Kravis Roberts (KKR). After a bidding war, the Boots board surrendered its independence and stock market quotation. The £11.1 billion buyout was the largest private equity deal ever done in the United Kingdom, and in many ways marked the peak of the debt-fuelled private equity boom of the noughties. Just a few months later in August 2007 the credit markets would freeze over, and the free and easy capitalism of the previous decade would be halted in its tracks. The takeover would also mark a landmark in the long struggle for pension fund rights to be recognised in boardroom deals.

Alliance Boots is best known in Britain for its 2,600 Boots the Chemist shops, but it also owns 400 overseas outlets in countries as far-flung as Thailand and Italy. The group was created in 2006 through a £7 billion tie-up with Pessina's European-based chemists chain Alliance Unichem, which supplied more than 125,000 pharmacies, health centres and hospitals across the Continent.

KKR's initial offer of £10.6 billion had been backed by the Alliance Boots board, headed by ebullient chairman Nigel Rudd and 96 per cent of the shareholders. For a while a rival private equity consortium, led by Guy Hands and including the Wellcome Trust and Terra Firma, also made a play for the company. Its offer of £10.8

billion lost out, however, after KKR upped its offer by £500 million. In the age of the corporate raider, just a couple of decades earlier, that would have been the end of it. Pessina would have been able to move into Boots' emblematic headquarters in Nottingham and do what he liked – strip the oil paintings of the founders off the walls, if he so wanted. However, Pessina's difficulties were just beginning. Despite seeing off his rivals, the affable but ambitious Italian was about to be cast as a public enemy.

The GMB union voiced its concerns, calling on MPs to tackle the practice by private equity firms of turning equity into debt when buying companies, a procedure that generally cost the exchequer vast sums of money. 'For example, when Boots is taken private the roughly £140 million Corporation Tax it pays will no longer be paid as the interest on the £8 billion borrowing to buy the company, but will be offset against tax,' it claimed.

But a bigger concern was the fate of the group's pension fund. In the past, pension funds, with their large surpluses, rarely received a second thought during a takeover. Things now, though, were different. Thanks to Labour, most of Britain's pension funds were in dire straits – their benefits considerably devalued. Trustees and scheme members were acutely aware that any change in the ownership status of a company could have a long-lasting impact on its pension fund. One only had to look at what had happened to British funds taken over by foreign businesses such as Danish group Maersk – which had wound up without warning – to be aware of the dangers.

The Alliance Boots takeover led experts to warn of the dangers to the company's final salary pension scheme. The fund, with 66,000 members – including 16,000 active employees still making contributions – was clearly going to be affected by the change in status. No longer was Alliance Boots in the public arena with a balance sheet supported by equity capital; it was now largely a debt-financed vehicle and the risks to the fund were much higher. Indeed, three years earlier, when Sir Philip Green had tried to take over

Marks & Spencer using debt arranged by the Bank of Scotland, he was chased away in part by an aggressive campaign headed by David Norgrove fought on behalf of the pension fund. David Norgrove later went on to become Britain's top pension regulator.

At Boots the first critic to surface was assertive former head of corporate finance John Ralfe, who had moved on to become an independent pension consultant, analyst and campaigner. No one felt more strongly about the Boots pension fund than Ralfe. After the tax raid of 1997 and the tech stock implosion, Ralfe had felt it was no longer safe for the Boots pension fund, with £2.3 billion of assets, to be so exposed to share markets. So, with the agreement of the trustees, the company decided to cap exposure to share markets and switch the whole fund into bonds. Given the appalling performance of equity markets in the first decade of the twenty-first century this turned out to be a brilliant decision. It allowed Boots to circumvent the big fund deficits which forced many similar-sized enterprises to close their final salary pension plans.

Ralfe, who was not afraid to stick his head above the parapet, feared that the high level of debt taken on by Stefano Pessina and KKR would undermine the safety of the pension fund he had helped to secure. He estimated that KKR should be forced to pay at least £500 million into the company scheme to ensure that future liabilities could be met. Initially, KKR and Pessina refused to recognise there might be a problem. Meanwhile, Alliance Boots chairman Sir Nigel Rudd came under fierce attack in the media for what might happen to Alliance Boots pensioners. Writing in the *Daily Mail* in June 2007, I was sharply critical of Rudd for 'abrogating responsibility towards pensioners and employees in favour of shareholders'. Rudd, a serial company chairman and City grandee, did not relish the opprobrium and a stand-off between us, later resolved, ensued.

Rudd, of course, was having to balance competing considerations. In a letter to the *Financial Times* in June he argued that if the Alliance Boots board had refused to sell until the pension fund issues had been resolved then it would have been shareholders who would have been disadvantaged because the cost of filling the hole would almost certainly have been deducted from the offer price. He sensibly went on to suggest that there should be new rules governing pensioner rights during private equity deals. In this the City warrior had an ally on the left. The TUC's Brendan Barber denounced the private equity groups as 'casino capitalists'. His objections fell into three categories – pensions and jobs, tax, and power.

Behind the scenes the pension fund trustees staged a stellar campaign which had the potential to derail the deal. Amid the furore, Pessina and KKR eventually made an offer to the firm's pension trustees of a £940 million package to support the scheme. It was to consist of an emergency fund of £600 million, which could be called upon in case the group fell into financial difficulty, and a further £340 million paid into the scheme over ten years.

By now the trustees had the bit between their teeth. Their response was to request a further £100 million, beyond the £940 million on the table, and an expedited timetable for payments. Trustees' Chairman John Watson was concerned about the implications for the fund of a leveraged buyout involving an astonishing £8 billion of debt. He also feared that, despite the defensive measures taken by John Ralfe, the fund had a greater deficit than its most recent valuation had revealed.

At a shareholders meeting at the end of May 2007 the trustees publicly attacked the Alliance Boots board headed by Rudd for backing the takeover while, they felt, neglecting the pension fund's interests. The trustees had no power to veto the deal, but City and pensions regulators were watching closely. Failure of the trustees to reach an agreement with the buyers would have made Alliance Boots the first FTSE 100 company to be taken over without the approval of its pension fund. It was not the kind of precedent that Rudd or Pessina wanted on their CVs.

The temperature continued to rise, with the prospect of the two parties facing each other in court. The trustees were advised by their lawyers that they could use a court hearing on 21 June to challenge the planned shape of the deal to make sure their members were protected. The hearing had been scheduled to arrange for Alliance Boots to cancel its share capital and transfer its assets to KKR. Generally such an event is an entirely routine event – it's a compulsory procedure that allows a judge to ascertain that all creditors have been fairly treated. However, the dispute between Alliance Boots and the trustees of its pension fund made it highly significant. If representations were made by trustees at the hearing, it would be a first.

At the eleventh hour Pessina and KKR, under mounting pressure, reached an agreement with the trustees. By the terms of this settlement the trustees would receive £418 million in cash over ten years, secured by a bank guarantee, some £50 million of which was understood to be cash up front. This was intended to cover the scheme's £305 million deficit. The long-term benefits for members were to be secured with a £600 million security package. The fund would have first claim on £200 million and would enjoy equal pegging with the banks for the balance in the event of insolvency.

Such power had never been given to a pension fund before, and it set an important precedent. No longer would private equity firms, or for that matter any other buyers of companies, be able to complete a takeover without some kind of agreement with pension fund trustees. The pensioners at Alliance Boots were fortunate enough to have robust trustees behind them.

A hidden hand behind the resistance of the Boots trustees was the chairman of the Pensions Regulator, David Norgrove. In a conversation with me for this book, Norgrove acknowledged his direct involvement:

Boots set a significant precedent because what it established was that the covenant of the company is a factor in how much money needs to go into the pension scheme. So the stronger the covenant, the less the pressure there is for money to go into the pension scheme. If you are weakening the covenants substantially then more money needs to go in. Leveraged buy-outs are something which are of concern because they increase the debt in the company and therefore the ability of the company to stand behind the pension scheme.

What is fascinating about all this is that shows just how much the pension landscape had changed in a relatively short period. In 2007 private-sector pensions were reeling and their trustees were anxious to protect them. Only a few years before, by contrast, they were regarded as prosperous and ripe for the picking.

Back in the 1970s and 80s pension funds were an attractive target for asset strippers and corporate raiders, who saw their surpluses as assets that could be looted and company contributions as costs that could be eliminated. The spirit of the times was nicely encapsulated in the 1987 movie *Wall Street*, in which the super-rich, totally unscrupulous corporate raider Gordon Gekko justifies his asset stripping to the packed shareholders meeting of a major paper conglomerate in New York. 'I am not a destroyer of companies,' he insists. 'I liberate them. The point is that greed, for the lack of a better word, is good. Greed is right, greed works.'

Corporate raiders were tough and ruthless. They used what became known as leveraged buyouts to ensnare vulnerable companies, either by buying into them or taking them over lock, stock and barrel. Since interest rates during these years were high, asset stripping had to begin as soon as the target company was acquired – not least to boost the share price. By the time the raider had sold enough assets to pay back his loans and interest, he would own whatever was left outright. As long as the sums had been done correctly, this residual value would be larger than the original sum paid, and his fortune was made.

Costs were cut by replacing executives, downsizing operations, selling plant or equipment, or liquidating the company outright. Company pension funds suffered because they became caught up in the financial manoeuvring that followed raids. Cash surpluses would be hived off, and the funds systematically dipped into or forced into default through company debts. The hard-saving workforce would be the biggest loser.

Corporate raiders justified their actions by arguing that their targets were companies with huge assets and low share prices that were not managing their money well. By launching a takeover, the corporate raider would either help the company to regain market confidence (thereby boosting its share price) or else liquidate some of its assets, returning money in the process to shareholders. Chief among the raiders in the UK was Lord (James) Hanson, who emerged as one of Britain's most successful and buccaneering businessmen. The name Hanson became a byword for all that was go-getting in British business during the 1980s, and in 1990 it earned him the title 'Europe's most potent capitalist'. He was the first British tycoon to earn more than £1 million a year and had a personal fortune estimated at £100 million to go with his reputation as the country's most-feared asset stripper.

Born in Huddersfield in 1922, Hanson made his start when he teamed up with his Yorkshire boyhood friend Gordon White (who also went on to gain a peerage). Throughout the 1970s and 80s, the two would target companies with pension funds that could be bought up, and then risk all to acquire them in protracted, often acrimonious, takeover battles. Hanson's all-or-nothing style defined the times in which he operated. The Hanson group assiduously acquired slackly managed low-tech businesses which still made steady money, such as London Brick and Consolidated Gold, and then stripped away surplus employees and product lines until the revamped business produced healthy financial returns and earnings.

Before long, the focus switched to the United States, with the group adopting the slogan 'The company from over here that's doing rather well over there'. White came into his own in this new market. Among the key purchases in the US were the typewriter and chemical conglomerate SCM Corporation, and Peabody Coal. Back in Britain, in the 1990s Hanson and White turned their attention to the utilities sector, buying Eastern Electricity, the country's biggest energy supplier.

Eventually the Hanson group developed into an £11 billion conglomerate that spanned everything from tobacco (following a bitterly fought takeover of Imperial Tobacco) and energy (the giant Eastern Electricity) to bricks (the housebuilder Beazer) and batteries (Ever Ready). At its height it employed more than 90,000 people. By the time the recession of the early 1990s bit, however, Hanson was falling from favour. He had been badly bruised a few years earlier when his daring takeover bid for the chemicals giant ICI had come unstuck, and some of the corporate excesses and failings of his empire – such as poor governance – had been exposed. ICI turned out to be a deal too far. Some went so far as to suggest that, far from being an entrepreneurial genius, Hanson was no more than an asset stripper who starved businesses of necessary investment, and whose success was built as much on the illusions of acquisition accounting as on management expertise. What's more, the new decade, with its stock markets on a bull run and its high-value shares, tended not to feature vulnerable companies that could easily fall prey to Hanson-style tactics. With typical aplomb Lord Hanson's response was to shock the corporate world in 1996 by announcing plans to dismantle his business empire, splitting it into four separately quoted companies.

What has come to replace corporate raiding in recent years is private equity – a more hard-edged approach originating in the 1980s. In the early days private equity companies were comparatively small-time concerns, making their money by buying less-than-sexy companies, such as engineering groups and equipment makers, stripping them down, turning them around and then selling them on for a tidy profit a few years later. In the 1990s they started to mushroom. More and more employers around the world have been bought up and then sold off by these leveraged buyout companies, which take pride in their lack of transparency, ability to rack up debt and skill at exploiting the tax code. They collect investment money from a variety of sources including pension funds, university endowments and wealthy individuals in order to buy listed companies and take them private – away from the stock market and public scrutiny.

They're rather less buccaneering than their corporate raider forbears. Their specialists show far greater caution, and the offers they make are conditional on board agreement after long and searching due diligence. Most deals are not backed by paper in the usual share-for-share swaps. They are paid for in the rather more old-fashioned form of cash, usually financed by cheap debt – a great conjuring trick of the noughties, when credit was free and easy, interest rates relatively low, and the financial markets found ever more ingenious ways of slicing and dicing debts and spreading them among investors.

Buyout firms are typically anxious to contrast their policy of taking a 'long' position with that of hedge funds, which typically engage in many more complex trading strategies – including futures trading, swaps and derivative contracts – and take 'short' positions when investing in companies, gambling that their share price will fall. Private equity aficionados boast that they invest in companies with the intention of owning and operating them for several years or more. The goal is to grow them, and turn them around or otherwise strengthen their performance. They claim that they create value by improving the operations, governance, capital structure and strategic position of the companies in which they invest. In short, they see themselves as long-term investors, not 'quick flippers' – taking time to strengthen companies so that they are worth more to future buyers.

Private equity deals grew 600 per cent in the five years to 2008. In 2006 alone £400 billion was spent on buying out companies. Today one in five UK workers is part of a company owned by private equity.

But with their successes have come concerns about the way they operate. Whatever they claim to the contrary, the turnaround in buying and selling companies is usually quite quick, and their ambitions are simple: to make as much profit as they can on the purchase and the sale of companies – and to extract value while they own them. On the plus side, for them this can produce up to a 40 per cent return on deals. On the minus side, for others it may mean selling off assets or firing workers.

The British Private Equity and Venture Capital Association (BVCA), which represents the industry, points out that private equity concerns are good at turning around ailing companies and making them successful, protecting jobs and pensions in the process. There is some evidence to support this. For example, when Nottingham University's Centre for Management Buyout Research looked at private equity deals in the period 1999 to 2004 they found that while there was an initial fall in employment by an average of 2.3 per cent in the first year after a buyout, thereafter there was a significant increase in employment – up by an average of 26 per cent after five years.

Pension experts and unions, among others, have twin concerns about the effect of private equity ownership on pension schemes. First, by saddling the target company with a large amount of debt it increases the level of risk on the balance sheet, raising the possibility that the pension scheme could go into default in future years. Second, private equity owners can always opt to make cost savings by downgrading the future pension benefits they offer staff. After all, they are in the business of offering high returns for investors and managers. Many of the companies returned from private ownership to public markets – such as the retailer Debenhams – emerge in a debilitated state.

The treatment meted out by KKR to some of the companies it has purchased over the years provides textbook examples of the dangers of private equity. KKR – Kohlberg Kravis Roberts, to give the American company its full name – is the private equity fund behind Stefano Pessina's buyout of Alliance Boots and one of the oldest and biggest private equity firms. It owns companies from Beijing to Johannesburg and Caracas to Bangkok. Through its portfolio of companies, KKR is effectively the second largest US-based private employer, and the huge fees extracted from deals saw the personal fortune of founder member Henry Kravis more than double from $2.6 billion in 2006 to $5.5 billion in 2007.

KKR came to public prominence as a result of the $25 billion takeover of consumer giant RJR Nabisco in the late 1980s, chronicled by Brian Burrough and John Helyar in the classic 1990 business book *Barbarians at the Gate*. When it captured retail chain Toys 'R' Us and media and market research firm Nielsen, its approach towards employees and pension funds became notorious. Following the Nielsen purchase, for example, it was announced that one in ten employees would be sacked and the company's US final salary pension plan frozen. It was all too apparent that highly leveraged buyers were being allowed to buy and restructure companies without being forced to honour all pension fund liabilities. What's more, the high levels of debt being incurred raised a serious risk that in the case of company collapse pension funds would be left high and dry.

Some measure of protection for workers and pension schemes in the UK came in the form of the 2005 Finance Act, which discourages the practice of selling off profitable parts of businesses to leave worthless company shells responsible for pension schemes with huge deficits. However, although collapsed pension schemes technically have the Pension Protection Fund safety net, the workforce of the stricken company still stands to lose out because PPF payments do not cover total losses. Moreover, because private equity companies (unlike public companies) don't have to divulge transactions and management decisions, jobs can be axed, pension rights curtailed and funds closed down in secret. The only defence has been negative publicity – hence the campaigns that have been mounted when the private equity cavalry appear on the horizon.

Unions have been vociferous in their criticism of private equity. The GMB, for example, mounted a clever and effective campaign against the UK-based private equity firm Permira, headed by Damon Buffini, over the closure of a clothing factory in South Wales. Pressure mounted on Buffini after he acquired the AA in 2004 and was alleged to have cut services. He became so concerned about the bad press that he mounted a high-profile public relations campaign designed to improve Permira's image. He pointed out that under the Permira umbrella the AA services were improved and that in many of the companies in the control of his group employment increased. Nevertheless, GMB boss Paul Kenny dubbed the private equity firm 'amoral asset strippers after a quick buck' – language gleaned straight from the 1980s and the era of Hanson. He also backed his rhetoric with research. The union calculated that activity by private equity firms had led to the collapse of no fewer than 96 pension funds.

The GMB called on MPs to establish how much in unfunded liabilities there were in 75 insolvent pension funds with links to private equity. Responsibility for pension funds defenestrated by private equity activity was falling on the state and healthy pension funds. The GMB estimated that 58 of those insolvent funds were in the Financial Assistance Scheme, and 38 under consideration by the Pension Protection Fund. Twenty-one of the funds had unfunded liabilities of just under £2 billion.

Pension funds too have staged vigorous campaigns. No longer are their trustees lackeys of the board or company directors. Trustees are now carefully interviewed and selected, and in the case of workers' representatives subject to election. Instead of rolling over when takeover tanks are parked on their lawn, they see it as their duty to protect the interests of the pensioners they represent. The days of easily moving expensive pension liabilities off balance sheets and exploiting any hidden cash or surpluses – a feature of the Hanson era – have long gone.

The year leading up to 2007 – when Alliance Boots fell to

Pessina/KKR – was one of unprecedented expansion for buyout firms. As the credit boom reached its apogee more money than ever was raised to purchase companies seen as underperforming, restructure them and sell them on. Fund sizes mushroomed, with £204 billion raised around the world in the 12 months to February 2007.

No target was too large. After the fall of Alliance Boots the grocery firm J Sainsbury plc came under siege in 2007, first from a consortium of private equity buyers which included CVC Partners, Blackstone, Texas Pacific and KKR, and later in the same year from Delta Two, a buyout vehicle backed by the Gulf statelet of Qatar. Once again the pension fund – first estimated to have a deficit of £400 million to £658 million – became the centre of attention. So concerned were the trustees about the fate of the pensions if a bid were to go ahead they hired a firm of consultants – Perfida, run by former investment bankers from Lazards – to advise them on how to protect members' interests. The fear was that in the event of insolvency future retirees and pensioners would be hung out to dry. Sainsbury had already taken steps to address the pension shortfall under the tutelage of the Pensions Regulator. It now raised £2 billion using its property portfolio as collateral and agreed to inject £350 million, in two separate tranches, into the scheme as an immediate fix.

But it was not enough.

When the Qatari bid arrived in October 2007, the pension trustees sought longer-term solutions. They demanded an injection of between £1 billion and £2 billion to ensure the scheme was fully solvent at the point it was taken over in a debt-fuelled deal. The intransigence of the fund trustees, together with the reluctance of the Sainsbury family trust, who spoke on behalf of up to 18 per cent of the shares, caused the deal to collapse. Lord (David) Sainsbury, the former Labour science minister who represented the biggest chunk of the family shares, made it clear he was not prepared to betray either his ancestors or the workforce. He remained concerned about the name over the door – not any buyer would do – and was also determined that the workforce and their pension rights be protected.

Clearly private equity and leveraged buyout players now faced enormous obstacles in overcoming the suspicions of pension fund trustees. Yet paradoxically the very same private equity funds believed they could be part of the solution for underperforming, deficit schemes. In a new twist to the pensions tale, they argued that by diversifying pension portfolios and placing a proportion of their funds in alternative investments – including hedge funds and private equity – lacklustre returns could be improved and long-term prospects for pensioners improved.

Stephen Schwarzman, head of US-based Blackstone Group, the world's largest private equity firm, was among those who questioned why unions and pension fund trustees were so suspicious of the sector. 'The high returns that have been earned over the past 20 years have been earned mostly for union-orientated pension funds, which allow for higher benefits for union workers,' he insisted. He was not alone. In March 2008, as the credit crunch started to cut off the supply of cheap credit to the private equity industry, Simon Walker, the savvy chief executive of the BVCA, told pension fund trustees at a conference in Edinburgh that it was in their interests for pensions funds to invest more heavily in private equity. Walker, a congenial New Zealander, had worked in the policy unit at Downing Street before taking high-profile communications jobs at British Airways, Buckingham Palace and Reuters. He was therefore a shrewd reader of the political runes. He knew the larger private equity firms needed pension fund money to demonstrate that they were working for the broader good not just bunches of rich investors. Pension fund investment in smaller venture capital outfits had long been encouraged by the government and the City as a means of providing finance to the growing small and medium-sized business sector. So the idea of a concordat between private equity and pension fund trustees – even though their goals looked to be so different in the noughties – was not entirely fanciful.

Among the ways in which a company can relieve itself of the increasingly expensive burden of running and managing a pension fund is to offload the responsibility. To an extent, greater regulation of the pensions industry has already helped to create this mindset. A firm such as British Telecom, for example, with liabilities in excess of £9 billion more than its assets, has to work closely with David Norgrove to ensure that regular payments are made into the fund and that the interests of shareholders and the pension scheme are balanced. Norgrove, a former Treasury mandarin who helped defend Marks & Spencer from the unwanted attentions of Topshop entrepreneur Philip Green in 2004, became chairman of the Pensions Regulator in January 2005. He inherited a staff of 280 from the organisation's predecessor OPRA and set up what he describes as a 'mini investment bank in Brighton'.

The first task was to set up a clearance process for corporate deals. In the past this had not been necessary. However, the establishment of the PPF – the strengthened insurance scheme for insolvent funds – made it more necessary to have some kind of vetting scheme. The authorities did not want corporate predators transferring risks in deficit funds from themselves to the PPF. Not surprisingly, the Pensions Regulator's interference in takeovers and mergers has attracted some criticism from the City, which has seen it as an unnecessary interference in the free market.

Norgrove, an intense, bespectacled figure, set up a system of triggers – using a complex mathematical formula – for ensuring that deficit funds correct their shortfalls over time. 'By and large I think we are into a different ball game now. That has had a major effect on the market raising funding targets and contributions, and accelerating recovery to fill deficits,' he says.

With the Pensions Regulator there to correct the mistakes of the past and keep an eye on the present, it's not surprising that an increasing number of corporations have sought to offload their pension liabilities altogether. As recently as the 1990s an occupational pension was regarded as an essential part of the benefits package offered by employers. By 2010 many companies were rushing for the door. And as companies retreated there was no shortage of free market capitalists who saw the depleted occupational pensions system as a soft target, out of which a new business could be created – the pensions buyout industry.

The buyout industry raised capital on the markets from rich investors. This new breed sought to turn pension fund management into profitable new business. It followed the model of companies like Resolution, the insurance vehicle built up by the buccaneering businessman Clive Cowdery, who in the noughties had made a fortune buying up 'zombie' life companies from financial groups who could no longer be bothered to actively manage them.

At the established end of the pension buyout business were well-known insurance groups like Legal & General and Prudential, with a long history of running collective investment and established fund management skills. A whole new buyout industry also emerged, including specially formed buyout vehicles such as Paternoster, Lucida and the Pension Corporation. The sniff of easy profits led even the shrewdest of the investment banks, Goldman Sachs, to become involved.

The way a traditional pension buyout works is that an insurance company takes over responsibility for paying benefits built up in a scheme. The scheme pays an agreed amount to the insurer, which takes on all the risks from that point onwards. The new owner undertakes to manage the scheme more economically and to invest the underlying assets more profitably over the long term. Ultimately, the same insurer usually provides annuity policies to each individual pension scheme member and the pension scheme can eventually be wound up.

So insurance companies swallow up the assets and obligations of closed pension funds and thereby gain access to massive pools of shares, bonds and cash which give them clout in the financial markets. Quite simply they amalgamate pension funds and run them more cheaply. That's not to say that it's all plain sailing. Pension buyouts are expensive. In most cases they require employers to add cash equal to 120 per cent of the pension liabilities on the balance sheet – a tough proposition, particularly in difficult economic times.

Nevertheless, as the noughties drew to a close the pace of activity was gradually increasing. In 2007, the year that the credit crunch hit, there were almost 200 deals done with a total value of nearly £1 billion. In 2008 at least ten FTSE 100 companies – including seven with schemes holding assets of £1 billion or more – were seeking bids from the pension buyout specialists for all or part of their liabilities. In March of the same year a report by actuarial consultants Lane Clark & Peacock noted that companies had offloaded £4.1 billion of liabilities to insurers in the last six months. This was seven times the figure in the preceding six months. In the first three months of 2008, 87 pension scheme deals worth £2.2 billion were carried out. Among the largest transferred was the £700 million scheme of gambling and bingo club operator Rank, which covered 19,000 members, about 10,000 of them already retired. This was later eclipsed by the largest buyout transaction to date – the £800 million deal to insure current pensioners in the P&O scheme.

The Rank deal marked the arrival of Goldman Sachs on the British pension buyout market. The buyout by the bank's subsidiary Rothesay Life concluded a five-month review by Rank, which in September 2007 announced that it was closing the scheme to new members and considering options for its future. Rank's two main businesses, Mecca Bingo and Grosvenor Casinos, had been hit badly by higher rates of duty, the smoking ban and the Gambling Act, which had scrapped big-payout gaming machines. Rothesay took on all of Rank's scheme liabilities, with all risk passed to the specialist insurer and Goldman Sachs ultimately to stand behind any problems that might arise. Rank collected a £20 million payment because of the surplus in the scheme.

In July 2009 the motor and household insurer RSA (Royal Sun Alliance) disclosed that it had completed a £1.9 billion deal with Goldman to secure payments to 55 per cent of its pensioners. The transaction involved the use of complex derivative contracts which neither RSA nor Goldman Sachs found it very easy to explain to shareholders or pensioners. RSA's chief executive Andy Haste, the man credited with rescuing the insurer from the poor underwriting experience of its past, was quoted as saying, 'This transaction further de-risks the impact of the UK pension schemes on the group's results and balance sheets.' He seemed to have a point, in that on some measures the pension liabilities of RSA matched the group's market value.

By now the trickle of companies seeking to shed responsibility for occupational pensions was becoming a torrent. Among well-known business names to offload their liabilities in 2008 were Morgan Crucible, TI and Powell Duffryn. In January 2009 the pension scheme of the former Leyland DAF truck company LDV was bought up by the Pension Corporation for £230 million. Leyland DAF, based in Birmingham and Lancashire, first drove into trouble in 1993 in one of the largest corporate insolvencies of the 1990s. The deal transferred nearly 5,000 current and future pensioners to the insurer, and Aon Trust, a trustee of the scheme, said the deal would make the pensions more secure. This was just as well, as in June 2009, after a series of failed rescue attempts, LDV was back in administration.

Regulator David Norgrove now turned his attention to these buyouts – and one in particular. In September 2007 the Pension Corporation announced its £400 million takeover of Telent, the rump of telecoms giant Marconi (the former GEC). Telent was essentially a small operating company carrying out telecoms servicing with a vast £2.5 billion pension fund with 60,000 members attached. Among the attractions of the Telent fund was an endowment of £490 million placed in an escrow account by the electronics giant Ericsson when it bought the larger part of

Marconi's operations in 2006. The Pension Corporation, a buyout group founded by private equity whizz Edmund Truell, moved to clinch a deal, but did so without consulting the trustees of the Telent fund headed by Chris Holden. In fact, they went as far as to replace the trustees with their own people and appoint the Pension Corporation investment managers.

The original trustees were outraged and protested that the takeover had 'created a fundamental conflict of interest', a view endorsed by Norgrove. As a result of the Telent case Norgrove went to the government and obtained new powers to prevent buyout companies obtaining control of pension funds as a means of benefiting themselves. The rules have now been rewritten. Norgrove says:

> There is always the possibility in any kind of corporate activity for the pension scheme to lose out. So it is our job, given that we have got these powers, to try to protect members of the pension scheme when these things are happening. In many cases we don't have to do anything because the company recognises its liability and deals with it properly.

The Telent case may have exposed the danger but it did not thwart the ambitions of the Pension Corporation or other buyout organisations. Truell's group would hit the headlines again in December 2009, when in the midst of the takeover battle for control of Britain's iconic chocolate company Cadbury it was announced that £500 million of pension liabilities had been transferred to the Pension Corporation.

Clearly, a cut-throat market was developing for pensions buyout. Among the more active practitioners was Paternoster, created in December 2005 by Mark Wood, formerly head of UK business at Prudential. Wood, who missed out on becoming chief executive at the Pru, started his operation with capital of £500 million. He had a staff of 107 split between the UK and India – where most of his actuarial team is based – and took aim at closed schemes. Paternoster boasted a glittering board of non-executives. It was chaired by Ron Sandler, the man brought in by the government to sort out Northern Rock in March 2008, and included one of New Labour's City favourites, Lord Leitch, as well as a former chairman of the Financial Services Authority, Sir Howard Davies.

Paternoster pulled off several big deals, including the buyout of P&O's pension fund and the £170 million buyout of publisher EMAP's scheme. It also became responsible for payments to Fiat and Texaco pensioners, handling some £13 million a month. In taking over more than 70 final salary pension schemes, it beat off competition from Legal & General and Prudential, which had previously dominated this market. But Paternoster was undone by the credit crunch. The FSA tightened its requirements for insurers in 2009, Paternoster found it did not have sufficient capital to expand any further. Moreover, its high-powered investors declined to stump up more cash for the time being.

Wood turned to his rival Truell of the Pension Corporation, and negotiations on a possible merger took place. But the deal fell apart, essentially leaving Paternoster stranded. There was no question, though, about Paternoster's ability to support the 60,000 or so pensioners on its books. The company had insufficient capital to keep writing new business, and Wood was replaced as chief executive in the autumn of 2009 as part of a major restructuring, although he remained as deputy chairman.

The pensions buyout market is a business built on the ashes of defined benefit schemes. It offers companies which have closed pension plans the facility to offload future liabilities on to someone else. Jonathan Bloomer, the former chief executive of the Prudential who now runs buyout outfit Lucida, believes it makes absolute sense for companies to part company with pension schemes:

It is risk management. Should you be running this block of assets and liabilities when your job is selling hotel space or making widgets? Do you really want the distraction? If you are a shareholder in a company do you want that? And do you want the exposure to equity markets and everything else that comes with? Or if you are a pensioner, do you want to be in a fund which has no capital in it and the only capital is the sponsor company, as Lehman's trustees found out?

Bloomer and other players in the buyout market make a good case, and tightened regulation means that this relatively new business is now more strongly controlled. In 2008 the government announced that in 'risky situations' buyout firms purchasing company pension schemes for profit would be forced to ensure that fund members do not lose out. The Pensions Regulator gained the power to require that uninsured companies taking over pension schemes stump up more cash to protect the interests of members. Mike O'Brien, minister for pensions reform, explained, 'I want to guard against pension schemes simply being treated as a commodity to be bought or sold. We need to ensure members' interests are protected.'

That said, there are clearly potential problems. When for example RSA chief executive Andy Haste announced the deal with Goldman Sachs, it was apparent that the driving force for change was the insurer and its balance sheet, and not necessarily the best interests of employers and pensioners. More worryingly, the terms of the transaction were so complicated that it proved almost impossible to explain. If there's one lesson of the credit crunch of 2007–8, it is that companies, even those in the financial sector, should not engage in financial engineering which they do not fully understand. And of course Goldman, for all its undoubted qualities, was not there to be a benevolent institution. Indeed it has a stronger instinct for profit than almost any organisation in the financial sector. A *Rolling Stone* article in July 2009 went so far as to suggest, rather uncharitably, that the bank was a 'great vampire squid, wrapped around humanity' because of its extraordinary ability to squeeze profits from almost any situation.

On paper, buyouts and buy-ins of pension funds might look like a splendid idea, and in the case of smaller enterprises, where managing pension funds has become a burden, outsourcing some of the work may make perfect sense. But the wholesale transfer of pension liabilities from larger corporations to buyout specialists needs to be looked at with a critical eye. My colleague Lisa Buckingham voiced her concerns in the *Mail on Sunday*. 'There are worrying signs that the buyout sector may not be quite as robust nor so ethically pure as could be hoped,' she wrote. 'Indeed, the Pensions Regulator has concerns that some employees are being encouraged to switch from defined benefit schemes to less attractive money purchase plans. The Regulator says some firms may be "seeking to avoid their full pension liability".'

At their worst, such private equity deals can seem to encapsulate the worst excesses of the insurance industry, in which 'zombie' life funds have been sold on several times and treated like pass the parcel. The fund founders and owners become rich on the proceeds but the returns for members of these poorly managed life companies can be lamentable and the degree of transparency and reporting abysmal. On occasion they may even end up in unsafe hands. The moral of the credit crunch has been, 'Beware of smart financiers bearing gifts.' Private equity, by its very nature, has a short-term time horizon and does not have the staying power to commit to an undertaking that may extend for 30–40 years.

Perhaps the biggest worry is that offloading pension liabilities means severing the bond between employer and worker. One does not have to be an advocate of old-fashioned paternalism to recognise that a pension promise – for example, what Tesco notably gives its employees – is a critical part of the benefits package and a great tool for building company loyalty. In the past corporations undertook to look after their workers in sickness and in health and to protect their retirement.

Thanks to New Labour, that had ceased to be the case.

CHAPTER 12

The coalition: a new start

On the bright spring morning of 12 May 2010 David Cameron and Nick Clegg stepped into the garden of 10 Downing Street to announce a coalition government which would 'take Britain in a historic new direction'.

The two fresh-faced leaders of their respective Conservative and Liberal Democrat parties were bringing to an end five days of intensive negotiations, which had begun on Friday 7 May after a general election ended in stalemate, with the Tories as the largest party but the Lib Dems holding the balance of power. The talks among the parties had been intense, with the Lib Dems briefly flirting with Labour before signing up to a deal with Cameron's Tories.

'We were all tired because we'd had almost no sleep,' declared the Conservatives' top strategist and negotiator George Osborne, the chancellor of the exchequer. 'But we knew this was a big moment, and we got down to business pretty quickly. My impression of the team that Nick Clegg had assembled was that here were four people of serious intent who wanted to sit down and come to some kind of coalition agreement.'

At the core of the coalition deal was a series of agreements on all aspects of policy from renewal of the Trident submarine to parliamentary reform. It was a relatively short document, filling just seven pages of A4 paper, but it showed a determination to dramatically change the direction in which 13 years of Labour rule had taken the country.

During an election campaign dominated by three televised debates in which the leaders were put under scrutiny by journalists and a studio audience, the issue of pensions and retirement – one of the greatest challenges facing any new government coming to power – barely received a mention. It was a topic almost too toxic to discuss. Most of the debate focused on budget cuts and restoring the public finances; little detail was offered on where the cuts would come from or on future tax policy.

Coming to grips with the public finances was above all the key priority. In Labour's last years, as a result of the credit crunch and subsequent recession, spending had ballooned out of control. The annual deficit had exploded to between £150 billion and £175 billion a year. As a result the national debt – the amount of borrowing accumulated over many years – was heading into the danger zone of up to 80 per cent of gross domestic product – the total output of the economy.

If this issue were not tackled the Conservatives feared that Britain's debt, which had a top rating of 'AAA' in the global markets, could be downgraded. Britain might then face the same kind of assault and forced changes in policy as faced the European Union minnows Greece and Ireland.

The retirement inheritance also required urgent action – in the private sector Labour's legacy was gruesome. A report from investment bankers Citigroup in July 2010 revealed the scale of the problem. The combined pension liabilities of Britain's FTSE 350 listed companies stood at £501 billion and their deficits at £72 billion. Corporate Britain also faced new accounting rules, which could slice away at earnings, and an increasingly aggressive Pensions Regulator.

The Regulator, with its duty of elevating the interests of retirees, flexed its muscles in negotiations with British Telecom and British Airways. A number of leading firms, including Marks & Spencer, Sainsbury, ITV, GKN, Diageo and Whitbread, restructured by moving property and other assets into the pension schemes in an effort to ease funding problems.

However, George Osborne's proposed change to inflation proofing, announced in his June emergency Budget, did offer some positive assistance. Instead of firms having to adjust payments on the basis of the Retail Prices Index (RPI), he proposed linking pensions (in both the private and state sectors) to the Consumer Prices Index (CPI) targeted by the Bank of England. At the time of the change RPI was increasing at almost twice the rate of change of CPI, which the Bank aims to keep at 2 per cent.

There was no doubt that the Tory-led government was determined to change the direction of pension policy. Osborne, the 39-year-old chancellor of the exchequer, was a man in a hurry. Tall, dark haired and aloof, there was a worry before the election that he might not have the judgement or intellectual weight to be chancellor. But the well-born son of a wallpaper baronet was politically astute and resolute. He recognised that speed was of the essence and announced his first £6 billion of spending cuts within two weeks of taking office. His first Budget – setting the agenda for future spending reductions and tax increases – came less than six weeks later. By 20 October his grip on power felt strong enough for him to unveil £81 billion of spending cuts to be spread over four years – arguably the biggest budget squeeze of modern times. And pension reform was a core part of his political ambition.

The switch of the basis of inflation adjustment from RPI to CPI, though hardly commented on at the time of the emergency Budget, would prove to be a very significant reform for private-sector pensions. Victims of Equitable Life, which had closed to business a decade earlier, were still waiting for compensation and the coalition was pledged to do something about it. The bill for public-sector pensions – including those of MPs – needed to be reduced. And sweeping changes were needed in state pensions.

The Tory-led government was prepared even to consider the bold change in state pensions that had been proposed by Lord Turner – and ferociously fought against by Gordon Brown – for a dramatic improvement in the universal state pension and an end to means testing. The coalition government meant business.

Equitable Life looked like a good place to start. Among the one million or so policyholders still living (tens of thousands had died still waiting for help) many were Conservative voters from the professional classes. There was a conviction that they should receive a better deal. At Number 11, shortly before the emergency Budget on 22 June, Mark Hoban – the City minister – told me that the government was not satisfied with Sir John Chadwick's inquiry (set in motion by Labour) and wanted to do better. He recognised the big gap between the aspirations of campaigners for Equitable Life and 'what the government could afford'.

George Osborne had recognised that Britain's pensions system needed to change long before the election campaign. Both in Parliament and on the stump the Conservatives had been highly critical of Labour's 1997 tax raid on occupational pensions and the way in which it had destroyed Britain's gold standard system of defined benefit pension schemes.

During his speech to the 2009 Conservative conference in Manchester Osborne renewed the attack on the tax raid, arguing it 'heralded the start of the age of irresponsibility'. He pledged to reverse 'the effects of Gordon Brown's pension tax raid and get our country saving again'.

In an address rich with promises of pension reform he committed to implementing Lord Turner's proposals in full. The pension age for men would rise from 65 to 66 in 2016 and for women it would jump to 66 in 2020. Public-sector pensions would be capped (in much the same way as tax relief for private-sector pensions) and there would be a more generous state pension.

Amid the horse trading of the coalition agreements many of Osborne's ideas for a shakeup of retirement provision remained intact. The final deal committed the coalition to 'review the long term affordability of public-sector pensions, while protecting accrued rights'.

In a masterstroke, Osborne fulfilled this pledge by selecting Lord

Hutton, the Labour secretary of pensions responsible for implementing the Turner report, to carry out the study. When Osborne delivered his radical spending review on 20 October 2010, Hutton's interim report was already on his desk.

The coalition deal also committed the new government to restoring the 'earnings link' for state pensions (another Turner proposal) by April 2011. There would be a new 'triple guarantee', under which the state payout would be raised by whichever was the highest of earnings, prices or 2.5 per cent – as proposed by the Lib Dems in their election campaign. Elsewhere in the agreement there was the promise to review when the pension age would rise to 66 years. There was also a pledge to end compulsory annuitisation – the requirement that retirement pots be used to buy an annuity offered by private-sector insurance providers – at the age of 75 years. 'Fair and transparent payments for Equitable Life policyholders' were promised as well.

Given that the pensions issue barely registered during the election campaign, despite the bitterness of many voters over Labour's retirement betrayal, Osborne was being exceptionally brave. Moreover, he was also recognising the reality that, unless fundamental changes were made to both state pensions and public-sector pensions in order to place them on a viable footing, there was absolutely no chance that the public finances could be restored to order during a five-year Parliament. The Tories were engaged in performing a great experiment on the economy – shrinking government and welfare to give business the space to expand – and failure would almost certainly mean them being trounced at the polls in the next election. Therefore the reform agenda, including pensions, needed to be acted upon with great speed.

Notably missing from the coalition deal was Osborne's commitment to reverse the impact of the 1997 tax change. Neither was there any reference to the National Employment Savings Trust (NEST) – the new scheme that had emerged as a result of Lord Turner's reform proposals. But the Tories would soon make it clear in government that there was no intention to roll back the clock on a hard-won reform, the battle for which had underlined the disagreement between Tony Blair and Gordon Brown in the previous administration.

The coalition's determination to get to grips with the intractable issues surrounding pensions saving was underlined on 28 October 2010, when the Lib Dem pensions minister Steve Webb announced that – after all the Labour delays – NEST would finally get the green light for implementation in 2012. Webb, a former economist at the Institute for Fiscal Studies and professor of social policy at the University of Bath, was that rare thing – a minister who actually knew a great deal about his subject. As of 2012 larger companies would be required to automatically enrol the bulk of their employees into a pension scheme, the intention being that by 2016 NEST will have been extended to everyone in the UK's workforce, right down to small two-person firms. Together, companies and employees would be required to pay up to 8 per cent into the retirement plan each year, although in accordance with Lord Turner's original proposals employees would be able to opt out if they so chose. The government estimated that the plan would bring between 4 million and 8 million Britons under the pensions umbrella for the first time.

The Webb scheme was not without its critics. The smallest enterprises represented by the Federation of Small Businesses complained about the 'administrative burden' of NEST, as well as the cost. Disappointment was expressed that 'micro firms' with fewer than five employees were to be included. There also was the worry, first expressed upon the publication of Turner's 2005 report, that bigger companies might use the excuse of automatic enrolment to trade down from their existing (more generous) defined benefit and defined contribution plans to the new NEST scheme, which would be cheaper for them to operate.

In a small concession to the less well off the coalition raised the starting threshold for NEST enrolment to taxable earnings of £7,500 for employees, against the original Labour proposal of £5,700. The new system would be phased in from 2012 with a joint company and worker contribution of 1 per cent, rising in stages to 8 per cent by 2017. Clearly, there would be much quibbling over the details and timetable of implementation, but the tenacity of Webb and the coalition in pursuing this once-in-a-generation reform was impressive.

As it had been for New Labour, Equitable Life was a significant problem. Labour never really accepted that it was its responsibility to compensate the almost one million policyholders, despite a finding of maladministration by the Parliamentary ombudsman Ann Abraham. Instead, it engaged in a series of delaying tactics. When it finally consented to compensation it sought to confine payouts to the most deserving hardship cases, on a basis to be determined by Sir John Chadwick. The ombudsman and Equitable Life believed that the amount of compensation required to restore the performance of Equitable Life savings to that of those offered by other major providers over the same period would be in the order of £4 billion to £5 billion.

On 28 July 2010 the former Appeal Court judge recommended £500 million of compensation: one-eighth of what was required. The reaction was predictably savage. Ann Abraham wrote to MPs urging them not to accept the paltry payouts suggested by Chadwick. She pointed to flaws in Chadwick's approach, adding: 'I thought it important for Members to know as soon as possible that the Chadwick proposals seem to me to be an unsafe and unsound basis on which to proceed.' As for the Equitable victims, they were suitably enraged.

Campaigner Paul Weir – director of the Equitable Members Action Group – who lost an estimated £50,000 in the debacle, concurred with Abraham. 'I agree 100 per cent with what she is saying. Chadwick is not fair or transparent. It's not justice. The bottom line is that we collectively lost nearly £35 billion. We are not going to be satisfied with less than 10 per cent of that.'

Chadwick was a Labour legacy and the new government's promise to heal the mistakes and delays of Labour was politically explosive. It would be difficult to find hard cash for one million Equitable Life policyholders at a time when the government was taking the meat axe to welfare programmes and removing child benefit payments from higher rate taxpayers. There simply was not enough cash in the kitty, and because of ten years of procrastination the pain could not easily be shared by spreading out compensation over a number of years; much of the sand had fallen through the egg timer.

Osborne promised to look at the matter again and then announce the coalition's response in his 20 October 2010 spending review. Chadwick was dismissed as too parsimonious and instead the government offered compensation of £1.5 billion, with payouts to begin in early 2011. This was triple what Chadwick had proposed, but only one-third of what Abraham had suggested and the society all but endorsed.

Weir and the policyholders group were decidedly unimpressed. Again they expressed anger and threatened further legal recourse. But it was hard to escape the fact that circumstances had changed. Britain was no longer the financially well-endowed country it had been when Equitable ran into trouble, and the coalition had gone further – as inadequate as it might appear – to address the concerns of policyholders in five months than Labour had in ten years.

The government also had far deeper structural issues to tackle. During New Labour's 13 years in power private-sector pensions fell into serious disrepair, swinging employment advantage in favour of the government sector. Labour sought to confront this problem but failed miserably in the face of fierce opposition from the trade unions – the election paymasters of the party.

The Conservatives were determined to tackle the issue, and fast. Lord Hutton, the former pensions minister under Labour who had stepped down from Brown's government disillusioned, was tasked to chair a formal probe on public-sector pensions. The Independent

Public Service Pensions Commission's interim report was published on 7 October 2010, in time for some of the proposed changes to be incorporated in George Osborne's spending review.

Hutton began by reiterating the importance of good pensions in the public sector, noting 'a compelling public policy objective in being able to recruit and retain the best possible people for these crucially important jobs'. He quickly became convinced, however, that there was a strong case – over the short term – for looking at pension contributions for public-sector workers at a time when the real cost of providing these pensions was 'falling on the taxpayer'.

Hutton argued forcefully that because private-sector pensions had been defenestrated it was not necessary for the public sector to go the same way. He described this as a 'counsel of despair' and made it clear he rejected 'a race to the bottom'. Hutton noted that the coalition's first move in the pension sphere, changing the inflation adjustment from RPI inflation to CPI from April 2011, would reduce the value of benefits by 15 per cent on average. Combined with other reforms put in motion by Labour the schemes would be 25 per cent less advantageous than in the past.

Nevertheless, the cost of public-service pensions stood out like a sore thumb. In 2008–9 alone payments to the public-sector pensioners and their dependents stood at £32 billion. This was compared to £50 billion paid through the universal state pension to all retirees. The report revealed the scale of the problem.

Cash spending on public-sector pension benefits was set to increase from £24.3 billion in 2009–10 to £32.8 billion in 2015–16, according to data produced by the new Office of Budget Responsibility. The Hutton Commission noted that the total liabilities of the public sector would reach just under a trillion pounds – £993 billion – in March 2010 (this despite the fact that liabilities were reduced by an extended period of low interest rates in the bond markets).

In his October spending review Osborne committed to public-sector pension reforms along the lines suggested by Hutton. He made a surprise commitment that the gold standard of defined benefit schemes would remain protected for government workers. The trade-off for this would be a progressive rise in employee contributions to be phased in by April 2012, with the aim of making savings of £1.8 billion by 2014–15. Other changes, including the interest rate at which benefits are set, would also be looked at following suggestions that they might be too generous. Clearly, public-sector pensions – for many years a political hot potato – had escaped rather lightly thus far. Not so MPs. Osborne was adamant that the most generous pension scheme in the land, that for members of the House of Commons, should be abolished and a new start made.

There was more radical action to come from a reforming coalition government with little time to spare. In Whitehall the arrival of the new government and a determination to end the welfare dependency culture saw Lord Turner's pensions reports of 2004 and 2005 dusted off and resurrected. Turner had argued that a fundamental reform of state pensions was both essential and could be paid for. This meant abolishing the second state pension, the means-tested Pensions Credit, and instead following the European model of establishing a more generous universal state pension. The scheme could largely be paid for by raising the pension age and diverting the resources from other state pension plans into the universal state pension.

On the eve of the Employers' Organisation annual conference on 25 October 2010, a leak of the government's big idea on state pensions appeared in the *Daily Mail*. Political editor James Chapman reported that the state pension system was 'to be given the biggest shake-up in 50 years'. The pension secretary Iain Duncan Smith would propose a 'single tier' state pension paid at £140-per-week, worth £7,280-a-year for a single person or £14,560 for a married couple.

This proposed change immediately drew criticism because of fears it would only apply to new pensioners, and not those on existing benefits. But pension expert Ros Altmann, director general of policy for over-50s service provider Saga, was broadly supportive. 'We still have the old system because of the mistakes of the past. We have to start somewhere. At least we can take care of the future if not the past.' Altmann estimated that implementing the change for new pensioners would cost an additional £750 million a year. But £200 million could be saved immediately by scrapping means testing and the Pension Credit.

A more generous universal state pension would move Britain more in line with countries like Germany that have generous state pensions but poor private-sector pensions. It could also encourage more private pension saving because it would end the bizarre anomaly (which destroyed Gordon Brown's stakeholder pension) that meant it was not worth anyone earning under £30,000 a year saving independently, because the pension credit would fill the gap. So, if it were to be implemented, it would be an incentive to save.

The coalition's proposed universal state pension reforms were far from perfect. They would be particularly unfair on women pensioners, for whom the retirement age was to rise incredibly quickly after 2016 to 66 years. This would be particularly harsh on women who have taken time out of the workforce to bring up a family. Nevertheless, radical reforms always create anomalies and it is not beyond the wit of government to create transitional arrangements to help those who are most disadvantaged.

In opposition Duncan Smith, the former Conservative leader, had become a radical welfare and pension reformer and the coalition saw his great reforms as a means of getting the state out of people's lives. Changes to the universal state pension were part of the larger plan and – paradoxically – also chimed with what the Turner Commission had proposed five years earlier, which had been rejected by Gordon Brown after a public spat with Number 10 over cost. Clearly the Treasury – keepers of the public purse – would still have time to stick a spanner in the works. But it is highly unlikely that the ideas of Duncan Smith would have surfaced without the tacit support of George Osborne, head of the spending 'Star Chamber'.

No one could have imagined the speed with which the Tories and their Lib Dem partners moved to tackle Labour's disastrous retirement legacy. In addition to the bail-out of Equitable Life and changes to public and state pensions, the coalition also uncluttered the tax allowances for private pensions. Under a new simplified deal for employees the annual tax-free limit for pensions contribution was set at £50,000 a year, allowing most executives to continue to make adequate retirement provision. But no longer would those at the very top, the boardroom fat cats paid the highest salaries in the country, be able to salt away large tax-free sums in their pension funds. An estimated 100,000 people who had previously exploited this tax loophole would no longer be able to take advantage beyond the £50,000 limit as a result of the new deal.

Undoing Labour's pension tax raid would be far more difficult in an era of deep stress in the public finances and would almost certainly have to wait. But in only a few months in office the coalition showed a willingness to tackle Britain's looming retirement crisis with painful measures. This more thoughtful approach – not all of it about saving money – provided a stark contrast to Labour's pension reforms, which had invariably shown a distinct lack of joined-up thinking. If there was a criticism, it was that because the retirement reforms tumbled out of government willy nilly there was no initial attempt to portray them as part of a coherent strategy.

However, Britain was finally showing a willingness to come to grips with one of its most intractable problems. Unfortunately, the gold standard of private-sector, defined pensions had long ago been ruined. And, for the time being, the government had rejected suggestions for changes in the law which might have allowed companies to consider 'hybrid' options that would bridge the gap between final salary schemes and more risky defined contribution or money purchase plans. Repairing the damage caused by the pensions raid was to be the most difficult challenge of all. It would prove all but impossible in an era of budget cuts and impoverished government.

Appendices

Appendices

APPENDIX 1

Glossary

Abraham Report(s) a parliamentary ombudsman report into insurer Equitable Life

ACA Association of Consulting Actuaries

actuary a business professional who deals with the financial impact of risk and uncertainty

annuity a terminating series of fixed payments over a specified period, usually the taking of a pension

asset stripping extensive cost-cutting by the purchasers of a company, who then sell on at a profit

AVC (additional voluntary contributions) singular occasional payments into pension funds

baby boomers children born in the post-1945 explosion of UK birth rates, coming to retirement in and beyond 2005

Baird Report Equitable Life probe looking at role of the Financial Services Authority

Beveridge Report wartime programme of social reforms which became the basis of 1945 Labour government's welfare state

bull run a lengthy spell of rising share prices pushing stock markets higher

Chadwick Report report into Equitable Life payouts

Chatham Chest seventeenth-century fund for pension payments to injured sailors

contracting out an individual's decision to opt out of the state second pension scheme and instead pay into a personal plan

corporate raid often hostile takeover of companies by firms who strip out costs and sell on at a profit

credit crunch heavy contraction in lending by banks and other institutions heralding or following a crisis

defined benefit *see* FINAL SALARY SCHEME

defined contribution a pension scheme in which the returns are defined by what is paid in by employer and employee and the performance of the funds invested

dependency ratio extent to which senior groups are dependent on younger working groups to support the state element of their retirement income

dividend tax credit the dividend paid net of a portion of tax, which is then used by the company to pay the Corporation Tax charged on its profits

DWP Department of Work and Pensions

earnings link a mechanism whereby pensions are upgraded each year in line with average earnings

EMAG (Equitable Life Members' Group) action group campaigning on behalf of those who were affected by the collapse of Equitable Life

escrow an account holding funds to deal with future contingencies/emergencies

final salary scheme (defined benefit) a company pension based on an individual's final salary up to retirement; in most such schemes benefits are calculated on the basis of one-sixtieth of annual salary

flat-rate contributions a constant sum paid by individuals and/or the government into a state pension

FAS Financial Assistance Scheme (for victims of company schemes going bust)

FSA Financial Services Authority

FSAVC (free-standing additional voluntary contributions) private retirement plans, used to supplement occupational pensions, attracting tax benefits

FTSE 100 shares index of leading UK companies listed on the Stock Exchange

GDP (gross domestic product) sum of a nation's economic activity

Golden Staircase Lord Beveridge's post-war idea of phasing-in pensions over 20 years

gold-plated pensions public-sector retirement pots based on often-large final salaries

Government Actuaries Department (GAD) experts in risk advising on the regulation of life insurers

graduated pension a second, earnings-related state pension

Granita Pact rumoured mid-1990s deal concerning the future leadership of the Labour Party agreed by Tony Blair and Gordon Brown in London restaurant Granita

grey pound/power/revolution retirees wielding financial muscle as a result of greater life expectancy and therefore greater numbers of older people

guaranteed annuity rates (GAR) Equitable Life's promised minimum rate of return on policyholder's investment at retirement

Hotel Group name given to the intimates surrounding Gordon Brown who met secretly at the Grosvenor House Hotel in the lead-up to the 1997 election

IMRO (Investment Management Regulatory Organisation) body partly responsible for regulating investments made by pension funds prior to New Labour's establishment of the FSA post-1997

index-linked pension a pension uprated each year in line with the official cost of living

leveraged buyout takeover of a company using high levels of borrowing

light touch description of the early approach to TRIPARTITE REGULATION post-1997

means-tested pension a state pension, the level of which is dependent on an individual's other income or capital

MFR (minimum funding requirement) a requirement designed to define the minimum assets that a pension fund needs to hold to meet its liabilities to members (replaced MFR)

MIG (Minimum Income Guarantee) a guarantee that then became the SAVINGS CREDIT and then the PENSION CREDIT

money purchase scheme (defined contribution) joint contributions into a fund which buys an annuity to create retirement income when the employee ends his or her career

MSR (minimum solvency requirement) a requirement that businesses ensure that their pension funds can meet their legal obligations in the case of failure

NAPF (National Association of Pension Funds) the trade association that represents the interests of private sector occupational pension schemes and plays an active role in corporate governance

NEST (National Employment Savings Trust) user-friendly replacement name for the NPSS and pensions account

New Labour preferred term for the business-friendly 1997 Labour government headed by Tony Blair and then Gordon Brown

NIC (National Insurance Contribution) the sum paid by employers and employees to the government, directly through the pay cheque, that theoretically sets the rights to a universal state pension

non-contributory pension company pension scheme in which a worker does not make payments, the plan being funded totally by the employer

NPSS (National Pensions Savings Scheme) a scheme proposed by the Turner Commission in 2005, later renamed the Personal Account and in 2010 rebranded as NEST

occupational pension pension paid by companies mostly with contributions by employee and employer and invested as part of a fund for the worker's retirement

old age pension state basic pension for all those aged 65 (60 for women) who have made National Insurance contributions during their working life

OPRA (Occupational Pensions Regulation Authority) precursor to the Pensions Regulator, established when OPRA failed

orphan assets extra sums built up by insurers on policies that have not been claimed on or paid out, and used by them for cash emergencies

over-bonusing Equitable Life's ill-starred practice of paying bonuses to match current assets, ignoring the industry-wide convention of doing so over the long term

PA (Personal Accounts) interim name for the low-cost state savings scheme coming into force from 2012

PADA (Personal Accounts Delivery Authority) the body charged with setting up IT systems and the investment funds required if the Personal Account/NEST scheme proposed by Lord Turner is to get off the ground

PAG (Pensions Action Group) the campaign set up Ros Altmann to represent the interests of people caught up in the wind-up of pension schemes

PCB (Pensions Compensation Board) inadequate predecessor to the PPF

Penrose Report judicial report into the causes of the Equitable Life failure

Pension Credit the means-tested benefit introduced by Gordon Brown to supplement the universal state pension

pension fund trustees body of volunteers, some of whom are elected, who make decisions on behalf of the members of an occupational scheme

pension holiday employers taking a break from contributions to company schemes which have built up large surpluses – popular in the 1980s/1990s

pensions apartheid perceived preferential treatment enjoyed by public-sector workers who retire on final salary schemes, while private-sector counterparts see their schemes switched or closed

pensions buyouts specialist operators using borrowed funds to purchase occupational schemes from employers and then making profits by running them more cheaply before ultimate sell-off

pensions mis-selling brokers and companies selling inappropriate pensions to individuals, often encouraging them to transfer all funds from occupational schemes into private plans

Pensions Regulator body responsible since 2008 for overseeing occupational pensions

Personal Account interim name chose for NPSS, the opt-out pension plan proposed by the TURNER REPORT

Ponzi scheme financial scam (also known as pyramid scheme) in which dividends and bonuses to existing investors are paid out of new business (subscriptions, premiums, etc.), not operating profits based on genuine investments

PPF (Pension Protection Fund) fund set up by New Labour to provide 90 per cent of benefits to members of failed schemes

private equity house firm specialising in using borrowings to take over target companies

quick flipping buying then immediately selling a company or home to make an instant profit; flipping has also been used to describe the practice of MPs moving their place of residence to attract higher mortgage compensation

Savings Credit the amount of savings permitted to people over the age of 65 receiving the pensions credit

SERPS (State Earnings-Related Pension Scheme) state scheme which ran from 1978 to 2002

SIPP (Self-Invested Pension Plan) a tax-free scheme, operated by private sector providers, under which people can save up to £1.8 million of investments for retirement purposes

SKI spending the kids' inheritance

SSRB (Senior Salaries Review Body) the body that sets MPs' pay and conditions

stakeholder pension low-cost government-backed scheme aimed at spreading saving for retirement

tax credit New Labour term for various forms of state benefit usually paid via the tax rather than benefits system

tripartite regulation financial regulatory system established in 1997, with responsibility for financial oversight split between the Financial Services Authority, Bank of England and the Treasury

Turner Report Lord Turner's 2005 review of long-term savings in the UK

windfall tax one-off tax imposed by government on a company's profits

with-profits type of pooled investment fund, normally run by insurance companies or mutual societies, generally producing higher returns and traditionally used to save for retirement or meeting school or college fees

APPENDIX 2

Timeline

1670s	First organised pension scheme for Royal Navy officers.
1762	Equitable Assurance Society – first insurer to be formed.
1908	Old Age Pensions Act – introduced first general old age pension, paying a non-contributory amount of between 10p and 25p a week, from age 70, on a means-tested basis from 1 January 1909.
1921	Finance Act – tax relief granted to pension schemes satisfying certain conditions.
1925	Contributory Pensions Act – set up a contributory state scheme for manual workers and others earning up to £250 a year. The pension was 50p a week from age 65.
1942	Sir William Beveridge published his *Social Insurance and Allied Services* report with state welfare proposals.
1946	National Insurance Act – introduced contributory state pension for all. Initially pensions were £1.30 a week for a single person and £2.10 for a married couple. Paid from age 65 for men and 60 for women; effective from 1948.
1947	Finance Act – limited the maximum amount of tax relief on pensions and the proportion that could be taken as a lump sum.
1959	National Insurance Act – introduced a top-up state pension scheme based on earnings known as the

graduated pension. Covered earnings between £9 and £15 a week.

1975   Social Security Pensions Act – set up the State Earnings-Related Pension Scheme (SERPS). Introduced in 1978, the scheme replaced graduated pensions. Rules for contracting out were also introduced.

1980   Social Security Act – link between state pension increases and average earnings broken by Margaret Thatcher's Conservative government. If the earnings link had not been broken, a basic state pension for a single pensioner would now be about £30 a week more.

1986   Financial Services Act – set out terms and conditions under which investment business could be conducted. Changes to contracting out.

1990   First signs of Equitable Life problems through 'over-bonusing' for policyholders.

1990   With fund valuations rising through a buoyant stock market, firms began taking pension holidays – a break from contributing to company pension schemes.

1991–2   Maxwell scandal: it emerged that *Mirror* newspaper proprietor Robert Maxwell had used about £460 million from his group's pension funds to finance his business dealings.

1995   Pensions Act – response to Maxwell, which set up regulatory and compensation schemes.

1997   Gordon Brown removed tax credits for pension funds on company dividends.

1997   Financial Services Authority set up to oversee pension regulation.

1999   Introduction of Minimum Income Guarantee (MIG) income support for poorest pensioners.

1999   Equitable Life sought to back out of guaranteed annuity rates commitment, but society collapsed after High Court ruled against it.

2000	Equitable Life crisis grew as it admitted £4 billion gap between assets and policy commitments.
2001	Baird Report into Equitable Life.
2001	Sandler Report into medium- and long-term retail savings in Britain.
2001	Introduction of stakeholder pensions, a low-cost pensions scheme aimed at people on low to average earnings and to help women save for old age.
2002	British pensioner Annette Carson, living in South Africa, failed in her legal challenge against the UK government to have her pension uprated with inflation. The case had implications for thousands of British expat pensioners worldwide.
2002	Switch from SERPS to the State Second Pension scheme.
2002	Equitable Life business sell-off began (but stalled short of full sale in 2008).
2002	Steady flow of firms closing final salary schemes either because of bankruptcy or because the schemes were proving too expensive to run.
2002	Pensions Action Group, led by Ros Altmann, formed.
2002	Green Paper proposed replacing eight pension regimes with one – a lifetime pot of £1.4 million for each individual.
2002	Pickering Report called for individuals to take more responsibility for their pensions and said measures were needed to encourage firms to retain final salary schemes.
2002	Government announced formation of Pensions Commission headed by Lord (Adair) Turner.
2003	Introduction of the Pension Credit, bringing 500,000 pensioners into means testing.
2003	First Abraham Report into Equitable Life announced (published in 2006).

2003	Number of firms closing final salary schemes became a flood.
2004	Financial Assistance Scheme launched with £400 million funding to compensate members of company schemes that close.
2004	Penrose Report into Equitable Life.
2005	Pensions Protection Fund launched as new safety net for those losing out when final salary schemes fold.
2005	Turner Report recommended series of radical measures – notably a National Pensions Savings Scheme – to ensure decent retirement income for all groups in state and private sectors.
2006	First Abraham Report into Equitable Life published.
2006	Pensions White Paper increased Financial Assistance Scheme funding to £2.3 billion and adopted many of Turner's proposals – particularly Personal Pensions Savings Accounts.
2007	Government agreed to compensate 140,000 workers who suffered when company schemes folded – they would now receive 90 per cent of what they had lost.
2008	Second Abraham Report into Equitable Life published.
2009	Government attempted settlement of Equitable Life claims, but legal action by policyholders continued.
2009	MPs' expenses scandal highlighted growing row over 'gold-plated' public-sector pay and pensions.
2009 (OCT)	Conservative Shadow Chancellor George Osborne proposed state pension age be raised to 66 years for men and women from 2016.
2009 (DEC)	Pre-Budget Report slowed introduction of National Pensions Savings Scheme.
2010	National Pensions Saving Scheme (aka Personal Accounts) rebranded as National Employment Savings Trust (NEST).

2010 (MAY)   Britain went to the polls and David Cameron's Conservatives emerged as the largest party in a hung Parliament. Conservative–Liberal Democrat coalition government formed.

2010 (JUN)   Lord Hutton appointed to head Independent Commission on Public Service Pensions.

2010 (JUN)   Chancellor George Osborne delivered his emergency Budget. He ordered that the basis for inflation adjustments on public service pensions be switched from RPI to CPI.

2010 (JUN)   Sir John Chadwick proposed £400–£500 million compensation for Equitable Life victims.

2010 (OCT)   Interim report from Lord Hutton recommended higher contribution rates for public-sector pensions but rejected 'race to the bottom'.

2010 (OCT)   Spending review proposed £80 billion of budget cuts over four years. Osborne announced government to set up a new parliamentary pensions scheme.

2010 (OCT)   Male pension age to be raised to 66 by 2016; women's pension age to jump to 65 by 2018 and 66 by 2020.

2010 (OCT)   Treasury announced new Equitable Life compensation plan, lifting the payout to £1.5 billion.

2010 (OCT)   Pensions minister Steve Webb let it be known that he favoured lifting the universal state pension to £140-a-week and ending the means tested Pensions Credit.

2010 (OCT)   Coalition government embraced the National Employment Savings Trust (NEST), based on Lord Turner's proposals

APPENDIX 3

New Labour pensions ministers

After New Labour took office in 1997, there were ten Cabinet-level ministers with overall responsibility for pensions.

Frank Field as minister of welfare reform (1997–8)
Harriet Harman as social services secretary (1998–2001)

The office of pensions secretary was then created in 2001 and its New Labour occupants were:

Alistair Darling (2001–2)
Andrew Smith (2002–4)
Alan Johnson (2004–5)
David Blunkett (2005)
John Hutton (2005–7)
Peter Hain (2007–8)
James Purnell (2008–9)
Yvette Cooper (2009–10)

APPENDIX 4

Pension examples

Workplace Final Salary/Defined Benefit*

Albert is a production line worker who started work on a salary of £25,000 a year at Midlands confectioner Sweet Tooth. Part of a Quaker tradition in the sweet industry, the firm is one of the last in the country to maintain a final one-sixtieth of his annual income. In each year that he works his pension builds up at one-sixtieth of his salary.

The employer contributes 19 per cent of salary and Albert chips in 7 per cent of salary. Albert works at Sweet Tooth for 40 years and his pension accumulates irrespective of what happens to the stock market and mortality. When he retires at 65 Albert will have built up a tax free lump sum of £135,558, which translates into an annual pension of £20,334.

His managerial colleague Roger on £40,000 a year can look forward to a handsome retirement having built up a pension pot of £216,893, which will provide a retirement income of £32,534 per year.

Workplace Defined Contribution/Money Purchase*

Helen is a pharmacist who started on £25,000 a year at the high street chain Head Cases. The chain abandoned its defined salary pension scheme in 2000, after Gordon Brown's tax raid, lowered employer contributions and replaced it with a cheaper-to-run money purchase plan. The employer pays 6 per cent of salary into the plan and Helen contributes 4 per cent. After 40 years of dishing out pills Helen will accumulate a lump sum of £67,663, which will buy a modest £7,496 pension income.

Maud, a part-time shop assistant in the same chain earning £12,000 a year will accumulate a lump sum of £32,478, which will buy a pension of £3,598 a year.

Personal Pension/Stakeholder*

Jack works for a firm of jobbing plumbers, Leaks Galore, which offers no pensions benefits and earns £25,000 a year. He visits a local financial adviser on the high street who suggests he take advantage of the low cost of a stakeholder fees and take out a personal pension. He pays an annual premium of £3,600 a year in four monthly instalments.

At the age of 65 he has built up a tax free lump sum of £54,897, which purchases him a pension of £6,092 per year.

National Employment Savings Trust (NEST)*

Florence is a carer working for an out-sourced NHS services firm. She earns £25,000 a year. There has been no pension scheme but the company is required to opt in to the new NEST plan. Flo is automatically enrolled. The firm pays in 3 per cent of salary and Flo pays in 4 per cent of her salary, topped up by a 1 per cent tax-free government contribution.

She is one of the 56 per cent or so of the population without any provision other than the universal state pension. If the scheme is implemented she will receive a cash free lump sum of £42,339 and a pension of £4,691 per annum.

State Pension

Pete, a builder at Crumbling Bricks Ltd, has paid his National Insurance contributions for 40 years and is contracted into the second state pension. He will receive a universal state pension of £8,000.

His mate Scruff has a broken employment record and decided to top up his state pension with a means-tested benefit. He can look forward to a pension of £6,760.

The boss of Crumbling Bricks, Big Sid, has been paying the self-employed stamp. This means he is only entitled to a state pension of £5,000.

Fortunately, over the years Big Sid has been investing profits in rental houses with the help of buy-to-let mortgages which have now been paid off. The properties bring him in a net income of £20,000 a year. This will be the main source of his retirement income.

*Key Assumptions

Fund Growth of 6 per cent per annum
RPI of 2.5 per cent
Earnings Growth of 4 per cent per annum
Annuity rate of 3.96 per cent (based on 65-year-old male, index linked with a 50 per cent widow's pension)

Bibliography

Altmann, Ros, *Planning for Retirement* (MetLife May 2009)

Amis, Kingsley, *The Old Devils* (London: Hutchinson 1986)

Barrell, R., Kirkby, S. and Riely, R., *Pensions Saving and the UK Economy* (NIESR 2005)

Beveridge, W. H., *Social Insurance and Allied Services* (London: HMSO 1942)

Blunkett, David, *The Blunkett Tapes* (London: Bloomsbury 2006)

Booth, Philip (ed.), *Pension Provision: Government Failure Around the World* (Great Britain, IEA 2008)

Bower, Tom, *Maxwell: The Final Verdict* (London: HarperCollins 2008)

Brummer, Alex and Cowe, Roger, *Hanson: A Biography* (London: Fourth Estate 1994)

Burrough, Bryan and Helyar, John, *Barbarians at the Gate* (London: HarperCollins 1990)

Coggan, Philip, *The Money Machine* (London: Penguin Books, Sixth Edition 2009)

Department for Work and Pensions, *Simplicity, Security and Choice: Working and Saving for Retirement* (CM 5836 June 2003)

Hollowell, Jonathan (ed.), *Britain Since 1945* (Oxford: Blackwell Publishing 2002)

Hutton, Will, *The State We're In* (London: Jonathan Cape 1995)

Keegan, William, *The Prudence of Mr Gordon Brown* (London: Little, Brown 2003)

Lamont, Norman, *In Office* (London: Little, Brown 1999)

Lawson, Nigel, *The View From Number 11* (London: Bantam Press 1992)

Lever, Lawrence, *The Barlow Clowes Affair* (London: Coronet Books 1992)

Magnus, George, *The Age of Ageing* (London: John Wiley 2008)

Norwich Union, *Pensions Uncovered* (www.aviva.com/media)

Parliamentary and Health Service Ombudsman, *Equitable Life: a Decade of Regulatory Failure* (HC 815 London TSO July 2008)

Pemberton, Hugh, *Britain's Pensions Crisis: History and Policy* (London/Oxford: Oxford University Press/British Academy 2006)

Pensions Commission, *Challenges and Choices*, First Report (London: The Stationery Office 2004)

Pensions Commission, *A New Pensions Settlement for the Twenty-First Century*, Second Report (London: The Stationery Office 2005)

Peston, Robert, *Who Runs Britain?* (London: Hodder & Stoughton 2008)

Pickering, Alan, *A Simpler Way to Better Pensions, An Independent Report* (London: The Stationery Office 2002)

Pimlott, Ben, *Harold Wilson* (London: HarperCollins 1992)

Robinson, Geoffrey, *The Unconventional Minister* (London: Penguin 2001)

Sandler, Ron, *Medium and Long-Term Retail Savings in the UK* (London: Her Majesty's Treasury July 2005)

Sharp, Alan, *David Lloyd George, Great Britain (Makers of the Modern World)* (London: Haus Histories 2008)

Slater, Jim, *Investment Made Easy* (London: Orion 1994)

Sorkin, Andrew Ross, *Too Big to Fail* (London: Allen Lane 2009)

Taylor, Corin, 'The pensions apartheid – can it continue?' (London: Institute of Directors, *Big Picture* Quarter 1 2009)

Thatcher, Margaret, *The Downing Street Years* (London: HarperCollins 2005)

Townsend, Peter, *The Family Life of Old People* (London: Penguin 1963)

INDEX